DUE

The Emancipation of Women

Nearly all of the problems posed by women's
liberation today were discussed *politically* in the German
labour movement at the turn of the century.
Thönnessen's book—the first major study to appear
in English—is a careful record of those discussions.
It also records the non-solutions accepted at the
time by socialist women.

Thönnessen warns of the dangers of *token*
equality which is all that capitalism can offer.

Werner Thönnessen

The Emancipation of Women

**The Rise and Decline of the Women's Movement
in German Social Democracy 1863–1933**

Translated by Joris de Bres

Pluto Press

Second impression 1976
This translation first published 1973 © Pluto Press 1973

First published in Frankfurt am Main 1969
© 1969 Europaische Verlagsanstalt, Frankfurt am Main

0 902818 26 0 paperback
0 902818 27 9 hardback

Printed in Great Britain by Robert MacLehose & Co Ltd,
Printers to the University of Glasgow

Contents

Preface

The book falls naturally into two main parts, separated by the outbreak of the First World War, which was a turning point both in the development of female labour and in the evolution of the German Social Democratic Party (SPD) and the women's movement.

In the first section, a distinction is drawn between three successive phases in the Party's attitude towards the women's movement. The first of these was marked by the rejection of female participation in the labour force, and is here described as the phase of 'proletarian anti-feminism'. It had its roots in the oppressive working conditions and the increasing misery of the working-class family, which produced an instinctive rejection of the existing situation on the part of the workers, although they did not express this in theoretical terms. There was still a direct contradiction between the tendency for female labour to increase and the protest against this trend: it was not yet realized that it would be impossible to abolish female labour given the level of the productive forces and the distribution of power at that time. The workers' attitude was determined by the traditional ideal of the family and the customary division of labour between the sexes, and they were unable to get beyond simply rejecting the new social development. Their attitude must be termed anti-feminist, for they not only rejected female labour under the conditions of the time, but sought to perpetuate the limitation of women's role to the home and the rearing of children.

The second phase saw the end of the simple rejection of female labour, for it was recognized that under the given economic conditions it would inevitably increase. The workers conceded that women had a *right to work*, and sought to eliminate the detrimental effect that female competition on the labour market had on their wages by incorporating women into the working-class movement and adopting the principle of *equal pay* for *equal work*. The first demands for the *protection of female labour* also date from this time. The majority of the Party, however, was not yet prepared to take a stand on *women's suffrage*.

After 1878, Bebel, Engels and Clara Zetkin set to work on a theory of women's emancipation, starting out from Marx's and Engels's concept of female labour and making use of their economic and social theories. They exposed the relation between the emancipation of women and the emancipation of workers, showing that private property was the significant factor in the past and present enslavement of both; they saw the emancipation of women as an element in the working-class movement and the victory of socialism as the only guarantee of its realization. They expressly stated that women's liberation was impossible in isolation. Their attitude to the employment of women was determined by the inevitable tendency for female labour to increase, and by a dialectical view of the misery that would ensue, which was not only decried for its devastating consequences, but simultaneously recognized as a force which would undermine the old social order.

The Party history of the period was overshadowed by Bismarck's Anti-Socialist Law and this brought the persecuted Social Democrats, both men and women, closer together; the prestige of women rose within the Party, and their connexions with it were strengthened.

After the period of 'proletarian anti-feminism' and the phase of 'the acknowledgement of women's right to work and the birth of the theory of women's emancipation' there followed a phase of 'the organization of women'. The Statutes of the Party opened up opportunities for membership and co-operation within the Party, a women's magazine was started up, and the demands for women's suffrage and civil and legal equality with men were included in the Party programme. The increase in the number of women workers brought a substantial growth in the number of Party members, whose links with Social Democracy were cemented through consistent education.

Towards the end of this period of organization, women increasingly became drawn into the internal Party struggle between orthodox socialists and revisionists. Signs of discrimination against women and a reaction against the theory of women's emancipation became apparent. Such evidence of decay stood in contrast to the numerical growth of the women's movement.

The second part of the book starts with a description of the opposing views on tactics which emerged in the Party at the beginning of the First World War. It deals with the increase in female labour during the war and the conditions under which women worked, and investigates how women's movements were affected by the split in the Party. The 1918 Revolution saw the most important women of pre-war Social Democracy in opposition to the Majority Party. The Social Democratic People's Delegates, who first took over the Government, introduced women's suffrage and wrote equal rights into the Constitution, thus fulfilling the two major planks in the socialist programme for the liberation of women. In the light of the continued, and indeed even stronger discrimination against women, however, it was clear that these legal reforms had no effect.

During the Depression, the emancipation of women was replaced once more by 'proletarian anti-feminism'. In response to women's expressed desire to share in political work, the Party opened up social work as a 'specifically female' sphere of activity. This shift in the goals of women's emancipation towards the right to perform charitable works, however important the latter may be in times of distress, merely served to perpetuate discrimination against women by other means. The theory of women's emancipation was replaced by a 'functional theory', which not only introduced equal rights, but went further to establish a monopoly for women in the social work sector, so that all other spheres could be preserved all the more stubbornly for males. The neglect and manipulation of women was demonstrated in the prejudice against female candidates for public and Party offices, in the question of appointing women secretaries and in the debate on the Press. The transformation of Social Democracy into a state-supportive reform party had its parallel in the metamorphosis of the proletarian women's movement into a training organization for social angels. The hints of a return to the socialist theory of women's liberation in Party discussion shortly before the National Socialists took power were no longer of any political consequence. After the forceful suppression of the Social Democrats, the Nazis particularly spurned their notion of political equality for women, while of their other demands for women's emancipation they took over precisely the idea of women doing social work, thereby exposing it as a means of preventing, rather than achieving, their liberation.

When workers make demands to improve their living conditions, capitalism tends to incorporate such reforms without any fundamental changes in the economic order. It tends to offset the pressures of the proletarian class movement by its flexibility in making concessions, thus maintaining its rule with even less opposition, and using the workers' success in achieving any given reform to weaken their demand for the transformation of society as a whole. This tendency, which has been described as the dialectic of the progress and decline of the working class, also played its part in the women's movement. By protecting women workers and introducing women's suffrage and equality under the law, the Weimar Republic fulfilled the most important demands in the socialist movement's programme for the emancipation of women. The fact that these reforms did not bring about women's liberation in practice was due to general political and economic conditions, for precisely with respect to the most important point of the socialist programme, the achievement of women's right to work, emancipation remained tied to the conditions of the labour market. Women's opposition to the social order, however, was thereby left with no ground to stand on. Because the women's movement had restricted itself to achieving the problem-ridden aim of legal equality, the existing society was able to liquidate the proletarian women's movement, which was pushing towards something more. Just as the working-class movement gave up socialism for the price of social legislation, women abandoned their emancipation for equality under law. The ruling order won out in each case by taking their demands for reform at face value, and proclaimed that the reformed conditions were the very best that could be achieved.

Section A

1 / The Period before 1863

In the pre-industrial epoch, the great majority of manual workers were held in bond by the feudal system (as servants) or by the guilds (as apprentices or journeymen). The free labourers of early capitalism were employed predominantly in the capitalist manufactures or in domestic industry. In 1800, there were probably fewer than 50,000 industrial workers in Germany; added to this were about 25,000 miners and quarrymen. Industrial expansion from 1800 to 1848 brought a massive increase in the free industrial work force, from around 85,000 to around 900,000. From 1820 to 1850 about a quarter of the total number of women employed were free workers. 'Throughout the first half of the century the number of women employed in factories rose in both absolute and relative terms; in 1816 there were approximately five times as many men as women in employment; thirty years later there were only three times as many.'

German industry, however, did not reach its peak of growth until 1851–1870. More and more workers became concentrated in the large centres of production. The percentage of women increased, particularly among day labourers and manual workers. In Prussia it rose from 12.7 per cent to 16.7 per cent in this field between 1849 and 1861.[1]*

There is little evidence to show any concern with the question of female labour, that is, with the aspect of women's emancipation most immediately affecting the workers, in the period before 1863. The constitution of the Workers' Fraternity (*Arbeiterverbrüderung*), for example, which was closely connected with the Communist League, stated that 'the question of the woman worker' was to

---

* References will be found at the end of the text beginning on page 167.

be dealt with by a 'special section' of the local committees.[2] In contrast to this attempt to draw women into trade union organization, the general tendency was for the statutes of the trades associations to forbid co-operation between men and women.[3] Subsequently it was above all the advanced section of the Saxon working-class movement which was to advocate the acceptance of women into working-class organizations on an equal footing. The explanation for this can be found in the nature of Saxony's industry, which mainly employed women.[4]

Nearly all the writings from the early period of German scientific socialism provide a relatively rich, although unsystematized, source of material on the early history of the family, the social role of the sexes and female labour. Such works include Engels's *Outlines for a Critique of Political Economy* (1844), his *Condition of the Working Classes in England* (1845), Marx's and Engels's joint works, *The German Ideology* and *The Holy Family* (1845–46), the *Communist Manifesto* (1847) and Engels's *Ten Hours Bill* (1850).[5] These works show that the socialist theorists were working on the complex later to be described as the 'woman question' well before the working class had even become aware of the problem of women workers. Obviously, the workers' attitude towards female labour depended on whether women appeared on the labour market as their rivals or whether they limited themselves to such branches of industry as mainly employed women. When female labour penetrated further than the expressly female occupations, 'proletarian anti-feminism' developed, which was only overcome at a relatively late stage through socialist education of the men and the joint organization of the workers of both sexes.

2 / 1863-1868

The material available offers very little information on the way in which the Workers' Association set up by Lassalle in 1863 regarded the question of working women. Lassalle did not discuss the problem at all in his writings, nor was it dealt with at the founding conference in 1863 or the General Meeting in 1865. The only resolution known to us was passed at the 6th General Meeting of the General German Workers' Association in 1867, which stated in point 4:

> The employment of women in the workshops of modern industry is one of the most scandalous abuses of our times. Scandalous, because it does not improve the material situation of the working class but makes it worse, and because the destruction of the family in particular reduces the working class population to a wretched state in which even the last remnants of its ideal possessions are taken from it. This gives us all the more reason to reject the current efforts to increase even further the market for female labour. Only the abolition of the rule of capital can ensure the remedy, through which positive organic institutions will abolish the wage-relationship and give every worker the full proceeds of his labour.[1]

Not only does this resolution still reveal a total bias towards the bourgeois family ideal; it also demonstrates the failure of the Lassalleans to understand the roots of the increase in female labour. In the *Critique of the Gotha Programme* Marx subsequently explained that wages withheld from the workers under capitalism could not be paid out in full even under socialist relations of production, for it would be necessary to make certain deductions to maintain and expand production and to insure against economic disturbances. Finally, some of the social product would also have to be set aside to meet administrative costs, to satisfy overall social needs and to assist the unemployed and those unable to work.[2]

Hilde Lion has described the standpoint of the Lassalleans on female labour in her well-known book on the sociology of the women's movement. According to her, they demanded remunerative work for women at home instead of in the factory. They recommended the men to go on defensive strikes to combat women workers who resisted, and through the exclusion of women from industrial production they expected to increase male employment, reduce unemployment and put up men's wages. The Lassalleans, says Hilde Lion, did not reject every type of female labour, but simply the employment of women in occupations 'outside the female sphere'. They planned to counter the efforts to introduce more women into industrial production by stepping up agitation among men, who with higher wages would be able to marry early and thus preserve women from the constraint and the attraction of earning money themselves.[3]

The Lassallean's attitude can be termed 'proletarian anti-feminism' for they not only came out against female labour under the capitalist conditions of the time but favoured the limitation of women to the 'female sphere' in principle, thus resisting the opportunities that were offered women to liberate themselves, through work, from male tutelage.

Luise Otto-Peters, known for her advocacy of women's rights during and after the 1848 Revolution, likewise forcefully attacked the Lassalleans for their attitude to female labour. According to her, the Lassallean principle that 'the position of women can only be improved through the position of men flew in the face of all civilization and humanity'.[4] Although she was particularly concerned with the interests of working women, the fact that the Social Democrats rejected the idea of female labour probably prevented her from working with them. In 1865 she founded the 'General Association of German Women', which advocated civil equality for women. Its members were later to be derided by the Social Democrats as mere suffragettes.

It was at the third Conference of the German Workers' Associations that the problem of female labour was first discussed in any depth within the German working-class movement.[5] Moritz Müller, a manufacturer from Frankfurt, gave a long address in which he emerged as the advocate of women's interests. At the close of his speech he said:

In short, we find a call to work for the greater education of women in every manifestation of human life. I therefore request the Conference of this Association to declare that in the case of women, too, there can be no real progress without the free development of all their peculiar faculties; that the intellectual element, which is independent of sex, must be developed equally in both sexes; and that the state has a duty to provide for sound educational institutions . . . The second point concerns the role of the workers in bringing about reform in the world of women. I propose two points in this respect. First, women workers are closest to male workers, and the latter must therefore educate the women on all questions of benefit to the working people. Second, male workers must bring to bear their full moral convictions to set the women onto an independent course. Hence it is primarily the duty of women workers to look after themselves, and secondly the duty of male workers to care for their female counterparts. As far as the individual types of work of which women are capable are concerned, most of these should be listed here, although there are others which I do not hold to be good, such as cigarette girls and the like. I suggest that our main principles be as follows: women have a right to do any job of which they are capable. Legal obstacles which still stand in the way of women exercising their rights must be set aside. The ability of women to do a job is not determined by whether or not they are allowed to do it by law, but by the fact of their doing it or not. Families have the duty to develop the natural abilities of women as much as possible through education, and the state and local communities are duty bound to provide facilities for the training of women. The workers have a duty to accept women workers in such a way that they will set up organizations on the same principles of self-help and association as their male counterparts.[6]

Moritz Müller then proposed three resolutions, all of which were adopted by the Conference with a large majority:

1   The Workers' Conference declares that for political economic reasons it recognizes the great importance of mobilizing female labour power . . .

2   The Workers' Conference declares that the true liberation of the female sex is that which leads to independence and the serious fulfilment of duty, and hence to the equal rights and equal status which must be earned by serious work among serious workmates.

3   The Workers' Conference declares that in future the workers'

associations must also assume the task of getting women workers, through education and moral and material assistance, to set up, in the same sense as the male workers, organizations of women workers on the lines of self-help and association.[7]

Müller's speech incorporated important elements of the subsequent socialist theory of women's emancipation: in contrast to the Lassalleans, who saw the complete abolition of female labour in industry as the only means of halting the disruption of the working-class family, Moritz Müller recognized that such a desire was incompatible with the economy of capitalism. He thus took up the ideas of Marx and Engels, who had seen the necessary connexion between the increase of female labour and mechanization. The inevitability of this process could not be stopped by philanthropic demands unconnected with the system. Müller made a vague reference to 'political economic considerations' by which he sought to express the fact that capitalism could no longer do without female labour. On the basis of this he demanded the establishment of equal rights for women workers and the liberation of the whole female sex.

With his assessment of female labour within the context of economic developments, Müller, the employer, came closer to scientific socialism than the workers, who at this time were still trying to preserve bourgeois family relations. In a paradoxical way, the roles were here reversed. The capitalist recognized the trend for female labour to increase and saw the inherent tendency towards emancipation, while the workers resisted any such insight. They wanted to eliminate the depressing effect of female competition on their wages and to keep women outside the working conditions of capitalist industry. The workers were so strongly pressured by their miserable material situation that they at first refused to recognize that female labour was a necessary stage in the development towards a higher form of society. Moritz Müller, in contrast, called on the men to lend a hand in the education and organization of women. He stated that female labour should be stopped only where it became detrimental to health. The Congress stressed that the further intellectual development of women would have a useful effect in bringing up children and in keeping the family together, for the man would be tied to his home and the woman would be in a position to share in discussion and action on all family matters. Other speakers demanded women's right to work in accordance with democratic principles or because it was the only way for unmarried women to make a living.[8]

The advocates of female labour were at a disadvantage at the Congress because their arguments derived from a change in social relations which could only be brought about with the help of female labour. They were unable to convince people by describing the necessary connexion between the present conditions of female labour and a free society. Their appeal to the workers for solidarity with working women was countered by the opponents of female labour with arguments about the seemingly unalterable, even deteriorating conditions of female labour. These people were unwilling to get involved in speculations about the role of female labour in the emancipation of the proletariat. They pointed out that the female sex was not ripe for trade-union organization, that the pressure of female competition was lowering wages and that the working class family was being neglected. Female competition, they claimed, could only be overcome within a production cooperative, and they could thus only support female labour in such a context. Frei, a delegate from Stuttgart, put forward the Lassallean thesis: 'Before we can emancipate women, however, we must first have fully emancipated the male workers.' The traditional argument of the conservatives was also voiced: it is sufficient for the man to work. The woman's place is to hold 'domestic sway'.[9]

The amazing thing is that in spite of the plausibility of all the reasons put forward against female labour, Moritz Müller's resolutions were carried with a majority.[10] After all, no official Party theory was yet in existence which showed the connexion between the emancipation of women, the disintegration of capitalist society, and female labour. Among workers, proletarian anti-feminism predominated. It was thus only great enthusiasm for the emancipation of women, even though it was not given a theoretical basis, which was able to make the participants at the Congress forget the personal material interests and prejudices that bound them to maintain the patriarchal structure of their homes and factories. As an explanation for this 'early discussion of the problem of female labour in male circles' Hilde Lion suggests the organized influence of a particularly enlightened minority (meaning no doubt, in the first instance Bebel and Liebknecht).[11] The positive attitude of the 1865 Conference to female labour was to remain unique in the early history of the German workers' movement.

At the Congress of the Workers' Associations in 1868 there was no mention of questions relating to women at all.[12]

After the establishment of the International Workers' Association in London in 1864,[13] its German section published a discussion document in 1866 which dealt, among other things, with female labour. It described the idea that 'the position of the female proletariat would be improved by drawing the female world into the trades, etc.' as a 'philanthropic dream' and spoke of the need

> to overthrow any remaining illusions . . . that it is possible to achieve even partly effective reforms in society as it stands, without shaking it at the foundations. . . . Bring about a situation in which every adult man can take a wife and start a family whose existence is assured through his work, and then there will be no more of these poor creatures who, in their isolation, become the victims of despair, sin against themselves and nature, and put a blot on 'civilization' by their prostitution and their trade in living human flesh . . . The rightful work of women and mothers is in the home and family, caring for, supervising, and providing the first education for the children, which, it is true, presupposes that the women and children themselves receive an adequate training. Alongside the solemn duties of the man and father in public life and the family, the woman and mother should stand for the cosiness and poetry of domestic life, bring grace and beauty to social relations, and be an ennobling influence in the increase of humanity's enjoyment of life.[14]

The vocabulary, which makes unembarrassed use of such notions as the 'cosiness and poetry of domestic life', reveals the reactionary views behind the radical gestures of the theory. Given the eminent significance of the stance taken on the woman question as a criterion for socialist attitudes, one can only note that a break has here become apparent between the denunciation of the capitalist system and the exaltation of irretrievably lost family relations.

One is at a loss to explain how this pamphlet could have been written by the International Workers' Association under the eyes of Marx and Engels. As early as 1848, in the *Communist Manifesto*, both had, after all, described the disintegration of the old family relations as an inevitable consequence of capitalist industry. They had written:

> The bourgeoisie has torn away from the family its sentimental veil, and has reduced the family relation to a mere money relation.[15]

The bourgeois clap-trap about the family and education, about the hallowed co-relation of parent and child, becomes all the more disgusting, the more, by the action of Modern Industry, all family ties among the proletarians are torn asunder, and their children transformed into simple articles of commerce and instruments of labour.[16]

The competition between male and female labour was also already discovered by Marx and Engels: 'The less the skill and exertion of strength implied in manual labour, in other words, the more modern industry becomes developed, the more is the labour of men superseded by that of women. Differences of age and sex have no longer any distinctive social validity for the working class. All are instruments of labour, more or less expensive to use, according to their age and sex.[17]

Eighteen years later, however, the German document not only failed to develop further the insights of the *Communist Manifesto* but did not even take them up in their old form. It used just those expressions which the *Manifesto* had denounced and which were also used by the Lassalleans, even though it was official policy to keep one's distance from the latter. On the level of the ideology of the family, therefore, unity was re-established between the two wings of the working-class movement, over and beyond all the differences in their political and economic theories. Luise Otto and Moritz Müller, as representatives of the enlightened bourgeoisie rather than adherents of a revolutionary theory, went far beyond these socialists in their knowledge and enthusiasm for the cause of women's emancipation.

'Cosiness' and the 'poetry of domestic life' also found their advocates at the First Congress of the International in Geneva (1866). The General Council presented a draft statement on 'female and child labour', which was one of the points on the agenda. In the precision of its distinctions and its feminist tendency it far surpassed the German document. The majority of the Congress, however, did not share this more advanced view. The draft stated: 'We regard the tendency for modern industry to draw children and young people of both sexes into the labour of social production as a progressive, wholesome and legitimate tendency, although the manner of its realization under the rule of capital is detestable.'[18] The draft drew a distinction, to the whole discussion, between female labour and its conditions under capitalism. By so doing, it was able to condemn 'the manner of (this tendency's) realization under the rule of capital' and locate the root cause of the new misery not in the rise of female labour as such, but in capitalism itself. The determining factor behind the draft statement was the insight, later to be argued in the first volume of *Capital*, that the foundations of a new social order were already present in the old society; which meant, in this case, that the liberation of women could not take place without quite definite preconditions, which also included the incorporation of women into the process of production. Since this was taking place under capitalism, there was an element of progress here despite all the ravages which were perpetrated at first. For this reason, these socialists refused to see female labour as unadulterated misery.

The General Council's draft, however, failed to obtain majority support. A French delegate (Coullery) gave the following reasons for rejecting it:

> The woman's place is at the domestic hearth, in the midst of her children, watching over them and instilling into them their first principles. A woman's vocation is great, if she is awarded her rightful place. If we free her from pernicious influences, she will be a pillar of democracy and freedom.

And a German (Bütter) spoke in the same solicitous vein:

> Yes, it is in the interests of both sexes that women should be assured of an honourable status. If, through a more rational organization of society, we make it possible for every adult man to start a family, prostitution will stop of itself.[19]

The fact that the central problem of women's liberation was not 'to assure women of an honourable status' and to abolish prostitution seems to have eluded the speaker. The actual extent of prostitution hardly explains the great interest with which Bebel, too, and the socialist papers, particularly *Die Neue Zeit*, approached the subject. It shows rather, that the socialists thoroughly shared the repressive sexual morality of the bourgeoisie. There certainly was a connexion between falling wages and increasing prostitution, as is shown statistically in Bebel's book. The significance accorded to prostitution in socialist discussion, however, probably springs from an essentially projective mechanism. The bourgeoisie were reproached for enjoying liberties forbidden to workers. Because the workers were forced to repress their own sexual needs, they accused the bourgeoisie of misusing proletarian girls and of not

standing up to the moral standards which they themselves had
been driven by necessity to adopt.

With respect to the proposition that the solution to all the
problems of female labour lay in marriage with a worker who
earned a good wage it should be noted that one of the cardinal
points of the socialist theory of emancipation was precisely that
women should be economically independent. After all, since
there was a surplus of women, many girls had no prospects of
marriage whatsoever. They had nothing to gain, therefore, from
wages sufficient for the needs of a family. To say that women were
to be assured of an 'honourable status' 'in the interests of both
sexes' was thus merely to paraphrase the old standpoint that the
woman's place was in the home. It was characteristic of the
bourgeois attitude still predominant among men that the speaker
immediately associated women's emancipation with the abolition
of prostitution, paying no heed either to the tendency for female
labour to increase or to the need to emancipate precisely the married
women.

A group of three Frenchmen vainly tried to rescue the standpoint contained in the General Council's draft:

> Lack of education, overwork, too little pay and bad sanitary con-
> ditions in the factories are the present causes of the moral and
> physical decay of women workers. These causes can be destroyed.
> All that is needed is better organization of labour, that is to say,
> cooperative labour. We must endeavour to make the work that
> women need for a bare living more suited to their powers, but we
> must not take it from them.[20]

This suggestion fitted the actual situation of women workers
and did not argue from some allegedly 'natural role' for women.
But even though it recognized that women were working for a
living rather than for pleasure, it was rejected along with the
General Council's resolution. Instead, a resolution was adopted
which spoke of women's 'naturally determined role'. Her place
was in the family. 'These are the services which the woman has
to perform, the work which she has to do; it is wrong to force
others upon her.'[21]

In explanation of such divergent views between the General
Council and the Congress and also among the participants themselves it should be noted that the International was by no means
uniformly Marxist at this time. It is true that its nucleus was
regarded as the most progressive organization within the European

working-class movement, and to a certain extent it was a matter of honour for every Workers' Association to be affiliated to it. Obviously, however, endorsement of the International's programme, which was a prerequisite for membership, did not mean that all the individual details of the theories developed by Marx and Engels were understood and adopted as well. It was highly significant that both Marx and Engels had experience of English capitalism, which was already highly developed. Engels had pointed to the importance of such experience of advanced economic relations for the formation of the socialist theory.[22] In Germany, in contrast, modern industry was only just beginning its upswing. This time-lag between England and Germany partly explains why the Germans were still caught up in pre-industrial bourgeois family ideals.

Naturally, both the opponents and the supporters of female labour claimed to be feminists. Those who opposed it could point to the capitalist relations of production and the conditions of work. At first glance it is hard to understand how anyone could have advocated female labour under the conditions of the time. In their discussion of work by women and children, Marx, Engels and Bebel all laid particular emphasis on the devastation that it caused. The misery of women workers and the neglect of their families produced a literature all of its own. It was proved statistically that women who worked in factories, and their children, had a higher mortality rate. Their families suffered and ran wild in their absence. In this situation, only a theory which saw history as a process was able to see that the ruination caused by female labour was not the ultimate stage of social development but contained an element which drove beyond: the unbearable nature of the workers' living conditions would awaken them to class consciousness and prepare them to receive revolutionary socialism. By getting organized, they would accelerate the collapse of capitalism. In this view, the misery of female labour bore within itself the seeds of its own destruction. Besides, the introduction of women into industrial production was the only way for them to liberate themselves from male domination. Dependence on a better-paid man would only have perpetuated the old slavery.

To people who did not conceive of female labour in this way, however, it must have seemed truly revolutionary to demand the return of the mother and housewife to the working-class family, and to demand higher wages for the men so that women would be able to stay at home. It must have seemed like the only demand which was sympathetic to women and showed a way out of the increasing misery.

The 'role of men and women in society' was also on the agenda at the Second Conference of the International in Lausanne in September 1867.[23] There were indications that attitudes to the woman question had changed. The person who gave the report on the subject drew a lively protest from the meeting for his patriarchal, moralistic way of speaking. The person who reported the procedures wrote that the speech 'sounded more like mob oratory, and indeed, on account of the theological outpourings, still more like a sermon, than a report'.[24] Even Coullery, who at the previous congress, had appeared as the eloquent advocate of the demure housewife,[25] declared himself ready to revise traditional prejudices.

> He did not wish people to go by past history, or to be guided by abstract ideas. Rather, the female sex ought to be assigned a role in line with its physical and psychological nature as determined by science.[26]

Even here there was still talk of allotting places and assigning roles. Quite obviously, women were still seen as the object of social manipulation by males, who now deigned to follow the principles of science, which was only just beginning to discard the myth of the physiological inferiority of women at this time. In the debate on education that followed, the father of the family was assigned the duty of 'bestowing on his children all the education they cannot do without'.[27] There was no further mention of the mother's duty to provide such education, for she was obviously considered incapable of imparting knowledge. In the proletariat, however, the state of school education was no better for men than for women. Earlier, it is true, the women's role had been defined as providing 'the children's first education',[28] and 'instilling into them their first principles',[29] thereby expressly limiting women's part in their education to the first years of children's lives. There was still a contradiction, however, between justifying the withdrawal of women from the process of production by saying that her real domain was in matters concerning the family and then saddling the fathers of the families with the responsibility for the children's education.

With the exception of the Conference of German Workers' Associations in 1865, therefore, the majority of delegates at the early workers' conferences took a hostile stance towards female labour and as a whole were more anti-feminist than anything else. There were, however, already isolated signs of a more positive attitude developing. The beginnings of such a development, contained in the *Communist Manifesto*, in the General Council's draft for the Conference of the International in Geneva in 1866 and in the resolution proposed by the French at that Conference, were carried forward by Marx in the first volume of *Capital*, which appeared in 1867. The most important ideas which Marx there contributed to the discussion of female labour were: 1. exploitation was increased by the fact that all members of the family now had to work (and thus produce surplus value) to support the family; 2. the proletarian family was being broken up by the women and children going out to work; 3. precisely the introduction of women into the process of production gave the working class the opportunity to emancipate itself. This was foreshadowed in the following words:

> However terrible and disgusting the dissolution, under the capitalist system, of the old family ties may appear, nevertheless, modern industry, by assigning as it does an important part in the process of production, outside the domestic sphere, to women, to young persons, and to children of both sexes, creates a new economic foundation for a higher form of the family and of the relations between the sexes. It is, of course, just as absurd to hold the Teutonic-Christian form of the family to be absolute and final as it would be to apply that character to the ancient Roman, ancient Greek, or the Eastern forms which, moreover, taken together form a series in historic development. Moreover, it is obvious that the fact of the collective working group being composed of individuals of both sexes and all ages, must necessarily, under suitable conditions, become a source of humane development; although in its spontaneously developed, brutal, capitalistic form, where the labourer exists for the process of production, and not the process of production for the labourer, that fact is a pestiferous source of corruption and slavery.[30]

Let us sum up the arguments which were given in support of female labour within the German working-class movement up until 1868. Marx and Engels had described it as a necessary consequence of economic development. On the other hand, bourgeois efforts towards the emancipation of women had found an echo in isolated cases, so that women's right to make their own living and to do any job 'of which they were capable' had come to be considered as a self-evident outcome of democracy. The Social Democrats took up both the concrete economic constraint for women to work, and the formula of women's democratic right to do so, which, although admittedly abstract, was effective in political terms. It was also recognized that qualified education and occupational training for women had useful consequences for the whole of mankind. At the Geneva Conference of the International the distinction had been made between female labour as such, which was to be encouraged, and the capitalist relations of production and labour, which were to be combatted. Finally, Marx had expressed the same distinction in *Capital*.

It should be noted in passing that the 'Democratic Alliance' founded by Bakunin also demanded the liberation of women. The second point of its programme stated: 'Above all we seek political, economic and social equality for the classes and individuals of both sexes.'[31]

3/1869-1888

When the German socialists met in Eisenach in 1869 for the 'General Congress of German Social Democratic Workers', the various statements that had been made until then about the emancipation of women were for the first time given a clear programmatic form. When the woman question was discussed, the two fronts, which we have already discerned in the period 1863–1868, re-emerged.

The Lassalleans proposed 'universal, equal and direct suffrage for men from the age of twenty'. The Marxists demanded voting rights 'for all citizens'. Their amendment was rejected by the majority, however, and only the demand for male suffrage was included in the Programme.[1] Female labour, too, once more gave rise to controversies in Eisenach.

> The men's hostility to female competition was expressed in a resolution which sought to make the abolition of female labour into a plank in the Programme. It was rejected, however, on the grounds that the goal it envisaged was unattainable, and that any attempt to suppress female labour would only drive the women who depended on their earnings in droves into the arms of prostitution. The danger of competition could best be removed by organizing women along with men, by awakening them to class consciousness and raising them to the status of equal comrades.[2]

Motteler, who was later to rise to greater significance within Social Democracy, made the following statement:

> We demand that women be given freedom of employment on the basis of a rational order, and that their abilities in the home and in public life be developed to the full. No slavery to the table and the hearth at home, no people disinherited of their rights

outside. The ideal of the emancipation of the female sex can only be attained in the socialist order of free labour. Hence the struggle against the present social relations, which are blighted by bitter intellectual and physical poverty.[3]

This Congress, too, heard the first demand for 'equal pay for men and women'.[4] All that went into the Programme, however, was the demand for the 'restriction of female labour and the prohibition of child labour'.[5]

The suggestion which had the most far-reaching consequences was that the competition of women should not be abolished by prohibiting them from working but rather by organizing them in the trades associations. It resulted from the recognition that female labour would inevitably increase under capitalism. After the failure to halt the pressure on wages by abolishing female labour, it was to be countered by the women combining into trade unions and taking trade-union action. In 1869, for example, the International Trade Cooperative of the Factory and Manual Workers of Saxony was broadened into an association 'for both sexes'.[6] The first German Weavers' Conference in Glauchau (1871) adopted Bebel's resolution, which bound all fellow workers in the trade to 'work for the situation in which women working in factories and workshops can enter the trade and skilled organizations on an equal basis, with a view to equalizing the wages of men and women'.[7] The Delegates Conference of the International, which met in London in 1871, also ordered 'female branches' to be formed within the working class. 'Obviously the aim of this decision is not to stop branches being composed of both male and female workers.'[8]

The question of the best form of trade-union organization for women workers was long a matter of controversy. In the course of time, there were both purely female trade unions and mixed organizations of men and women, and finally there were women's alliances which were affiliated corporately to the male trade unions. The socialist women waged a campaign against the bourgeois women's movement, attacking its class nature and its sentimental philanthropy, but this forced them to abandon the principle of purely female trade unions, for such unions spoke for 'women' rather than for 'women proletarians'. The image of the 'lady' or the 'woman' which was cultivated in them was derided by the socialists as bourgeois ideology, although the fear of competition from the bourgeois women's organizations undoubtedly played no small part in their campaign. Just when the working-class movement was beginning to put the principle of joint organization for men and women into practice, and women were starting to join the trade unions on a larger scale, the Combination Laws forced them to form separate organizations once more. This situation lasted until 1908.[9]

At the time when agitation among women workers was at its height (approximately 1898–1913), it was not only legal regulations which encouraged women to establish a separate movement. A further justification was the fact that the women's movement had the special task of finding out ways and means of making socialism 'more comprehensible to the masses of proletarian women, and of drawing them into conscious cooperation'.[10]

> If they (the women comrades) wanted to bring socialism to the mass of proletarian women, they had to take into account these women's political backwardness, their emotional peculiarities, their two-fold burden at home and in the factory, in short, all the special features of their existence, actions, feelings and thoughts. Accordingly, they had in part to adopt different ways and means in their work, and seek other points of contact, than the male comrades did in their educational and organizational work among the male proletariat.[11]

Clara Zetkin put forward similar arguments in all her writings.[12] The special tasks of the women's movement explain why the women retained certain special rights even after their amalgamation with the general organizations.

It is true that the Social Democratic Conferences of 1870/1871 did not discuss women's questions. However, enough other documents exist to distinguish the opposing fronts in the question of female labour until about 1875, the founding year of the United Social Democratic Workers' Party. The workers who thought in trade union terms were strictly opposed to female labour. In 1872, for example, the Erfurt Workers' Congress resolved 'to work against all female labour in the factories and workshops and to abolish the same'.[13]

The trade unions' attitude towards female labour reveals their direct orientation towards improving the worker's material living conditions, which for some time constituted the specific difference between them and Social Democracy. Whereas, at least in theory, the political party aimed at the overthrow of capitalist society, the trade unions concentrated their thinking on bettering conditions of work. The emphasis of trade-union organization lay in the wages struggle, the reduction of working hours and, in very broad terms, on social legislation based on the existing order. This difference only disappeared when the trade-union wing of the working class movement was strengthened. The predominance of the trade unions meant that Social Democracy became increasingly oriented on the achievement of social reforms.

There was very little difference between the attitude of the trade unions and the following comments in *Der Volksstaat*, the 'Organ of the Social Democratic Workers' Party and the International Trade Union Cooperatives', which appeared in 1873:

> There are no objections to female and child labour in themselves, and Owen even regarded the latter as an integrative aspect of young people's education. But we are concerned with the contemporary mode of production, not with an ideal state which must be striven for; and as things stand at present, we must support every measure which aims to restrict women and children from working and to regulate the sanitary conditions of such work. Indeed, as long as capitalism continues to rule, we have an obligation to strive to keep women and children out of bourgeois industry altogether, both in the interests of the women and children themselves, and in the interests of the proletariat in general.[14]

Nevertheless, this statement must be attributed to an advance in political consciousness, for it took a positive attitude to female labour, even if it did support it only in a socialist society. On the other hand, it failed to understand the way in which the very fact of female labour contributed to the achievement of the 'ideal state, which must be striven for', and created the conditions in which the idea of women working was given support. Furthermore, the feeling of obligation 'to keep women and children out of bourgeois industry altogether' indicated that the article was not conscious of the contradiction between such a demand and the state of the productive forces and relationships of power at the time. The gap between this statement and the most progressive standpoint of the socialists was thus still very great. The socialists supported female labour because it was inevitable under capitalism, seeing it as a means of emancipating women and as a destructive principle of the old society. They fought to improve women's working conditions in the conviction that this would bring in its wake an improvement in the working conditions of the workforce as a whole.

In the attitudes of the trade unions, the *Volksstaat* and the Marxists towards female labour we can discern three different stages of the development of the working-class movement. Because of their lack of theory, the trade unions went no further than to reject the status quo and therefore precisely conformed to it, since they did not know how to combat it effectively. The workers who had already been influenced by Social Democracy differentiated between female labour and capitalism, while the socialist theorists took the dialectical position described above.

For the Unification Conference of the Lassallean and Eisenach Parties, which took place in Gotha in May 1875, a draft programme had been worked out, which under Point II, 1, foresaw 'equal, direct and secret suffrage for all men over 21 in all local and national elections', and under Point III, 3, 'the restriction of female labour and the prohibition of child labour'.[15]

Various groups proposed amendments to both points. The conservatives wanted to 'prohibit' rather than 'restrict' female labour,[16] the progressives demanded the suffrage for 'citizens of both sexes'.[17] In a speech justifying his proposed amendment, Wilhelm Liebknecht said:

> Admittedly, opponents of female suffrage often maintain that women have no political education. But there are plenty of men in the same position, and by this reasoning they ought not to be allowed to vote either. The 'herd of voters' which has figured at all the elections did not consist of women. A party which has inscribed 'equality' on its banner flies in the face of its own words if it denies political rights to half of the human race.[18]

Hasselmann asked people to remember that women, with their inadequate education, might well give their votes to the reactionaries. When women were in fact given the suffrage in the Weimar Republic these fears were partly borne out. Bebel, however, met Hasselmann's objections by saying that one must strive to educate the women. 'And this is done precisely by giving them the right to vote, so that they obtain practice in using the same.'[19] Bebel's amendment proposing 'the right to vote for citizens of both sexes' was nonetheless rejected by 62 votes to 55, and instead 'general equal and direct suffrage with secret and obligatory voting for all citizens over 20 years of age' was included in the Programme.[20]

This compromise avoided, on the one hand, any explicit mention of women, but permitted them, on the other, to be included under the concept of 'citizens'. The first amendment, which demanded the prohibition of female labour in industry, was rejected by a majority, as it had already been in Eisenach, and the draft programme was altered to demand the 'prohibition of child labour and of all female labour which is morally or physically detrimental'.[21]

Marx, who later criticized the draft programme rather than the version adopted at Gotha, wrote something similar on this point:

> The standardization of the working day must include the restriction of female labour, in so far as it relates to the duration, intermissions, etc, of the working day; otherwise it could only mean the exclusion of female labour from branches of industry that are especially unhealthy for the female body or objectionable morally for the female sex.[22]

Both the concept of 'morally detrimental' in the Gotha Programme and of 'objectionable morally' in Marx's critique show that the socialists were letting their standard of morality be prescribed by the ruling attitudes of the bourgeoisie. This is all the more amazing, as Marx had pointed out in the *Communist Manifesto* that all moral relations in the proletariat flew in the face of bourgeois morals.

Female labour in industry as a whole was incompatible with the bourgeois ideal of the family. If then, particular instances of 'morally objectionable' female labour were to be prohibited over and above this, then admittedly, given the fact that jobs detrimental to health were mentioned separately in the demand for protection, it was possible to think of jobs which were incompatible with the concept of 'femininity' as held by the bourgeoisie, but obviously shared by the socialists. Bebel, for example, wrote:

> It is truly not a lovely sight to see women, even with child, vying with men in wheeling heavily laden barrows on railway construction sites; or to observe them mixing lime and cement, or carrying heavy loads, or stones, as labourers on building sites, or to see them working at washing coal or ironstone. The women there are stripped of all that is feminine and their femininity is trampled under foot, just as our men, in many different types of employment, are bereft of anything manly.[23]

B

In the case of women, such work could be distinguished only with difficulty from jobs detrimental to health. What was morally objectionable, however, was obviously the use of women in the pleasure business, for the femininity which put itself up for show in precisely this sphere aroused Bebel to even greater indignation than the loss of femininity in heavy or dirty labour. He wrote:

> Finally, younger and especially prettier women are used more and more, with the greatest damage to their whole personality, in all manner of public haunts as service personnel, singers, dancers, and so on, for the enticement of the pleasure-hungry male world. This area is governed by the most loathsome abuses and the white slave-owners here celebrate their wildest orgies.[24]

The concept of moral objectionability, therefore, included not only those activities which, as a result of the physical demands they made, could just as well be included among those damaging to health, but also moral indignation at female occupations which sinned against the bourgeois ideals of purity and chastity. And indeed, the tenor of the accusations became all the more strident, the more the bourgeoisie seemed to do injury to its own morals, which the socialists would have liked to take seriously. Here, as in the discussion on prostitution, we see the socialists' condemnatory judgments to be the result of repression and projection—the product of a sexual morality which they had taken over from the bourgeoisie without any compensatory share in the bourgeoisie's freedom.

A comparison of the discussion about women's liberation within the Party and the measures demanded by the Social Democrats in the political forum, the Reichstag, reveals that the protection of women was not demanded until 1877 and female suffrage not until 1895. An even greater period separates the time when the Social Democrats first presented these demands and their actual realization through legislation. An improvement in the protection of women workers was granted in 1891, and women did not receive the vote until the 1918 Revolution. We must make a distinction between

1   the clarification of attitudes towards women's emancipation within Social Democracy itself;
2   the formulation of corresponding demands to the legislators; and
3   their realization through Act of Parliament.

The position now taken by the Party, which in the political sphere was expressed in the very imprecise demand for equal voting rights for both sexes, and in the economic sphere in support for female labour with rational restrictions, remained unchanged until 1889. As early as 1876, however, there were signs of second thoughts about workers' protection. At the Gotha Socialist Congress, Kapell said that the Party Programme constituted the only law for workers' protection, and that it was wrong to demand palliative measures along these lines from the contemporary state.[25] He seems to have recognized at a very early stage the contradiction which arose from the opposition of the working class to capitalism in principle and the constraint to reform the system, which would obscure class antagonisms. He had a premonition of the contradiction that this would produce between the rise of the working-class movement through the partial achievement of its demands for reform, and its decline through the weakening of class consciousness despite the continuance of exploitation. The fact that, with the development of social legislation, capitalism would change its methods but would certainly not be abolished, only entered the general consciousness much later.

In practice, Social Democracy paved the way for workers' protection. In 1877, the twelve Social Democratic Members of Parliament, with the backing of four bourgeois representatives, introduced the first bill for workers' protection. As late as the Halle Party Conference in 1890 it was still claimed that workers' protection would enable the workers to take an active part in the class struggle. 'The more we raise the living conditions of the worker, the more will our army grow, and the more will it become strong in its actions, determined in its aims, and powerful in its ability to strike.'[26] Developments were to refute this prognosis, for they took precisely the course of the dialectic of rise and decline described above.

In 1882, in Rouanne, an amendment was made to the 'minimum programme' of the French Workers' Party, which had been worked out by Marx, Engels, Guesde and Lafargue in 1880. A legal measure was added there to the economic and political demands for women's emancipation: 'The abolition of all paragraphs of law which . . . put women in a subordinate position to men.'[27]

The themes were thus expressed which were later to produce, in summary form, the Social Democratic programme for the emancipation of women. There was clarity about the need for the protection of women workers. There were demands for women's right to vote and for legal equality, although admittedly the latter was only taken up in 1891 in the Erfurt Programme of Social Democracy.

The period from 1878 to 1890 was completely overshadowed by the Exceptional Law against Social Democracy. All Party organs were prohibited, and the leadership was transferred to the Social Democratic caucus in the Reichstag. The German Socialists were forced to hold their conferences abroad. In 1880 they met at Schloss Wyden in Switzerland, in 1883 in Copenhagen, and in 1887 in St Gallen. Women questions, in particular, were not dealt with at these conferences.

Although the political activity of German Social Democracy was almost totally paralysed in the period of the Anti-Socialist Law, there were nonetheless two events of note in the literary sphere. The year 1878 saw the publication of the first book to attempt to investigate the woman question as a whole from a socialist viewpoint. It was August Bebel's *Woman in the Past, Present and Future*. The book was later renamed *Die Frau und der Sozialismus* (Woman and Socialism), and went into 58 editions in the German language, of which fifty alone appeared between 1879 and 1909. It was also translated into many foreign languages. Bebel's book first appeared in Leipzig, under a deliberately misleading title, only a few months after the Anti-Socialist Law had been passed, and subsequent editions of about 15,000 were published in Zurich. From there they were smuggled into Germany along with the Party newspaper *Sozialdemokrat*, with the aid of an organization of agents called the 'Red Fieldpost'.[28] Bebel undertook numerous alterations and additions for the new editions, and gave detailed replies to criticisms made by eugenicists, ethnologists and sexologists. Apart from such people, the book also received recognition among academics. Bebel dealt with the development of women's status from primitive society up to the bourgeois family, and discussed the sexual relations and social relations of marriage predominant in his own time, prostitution, female labour and equal rights. His description of primitive society, promiscuity and the origins of monogamy, would today be regarded as outmoded.

Bebel's central thesis, however, that economic development was the cause of women's suppression, does not lose any of its validity through this. In explaining the transition to monogamy,

Bebel does admittedly often project bourgeois motives and relations on to earlier historical epochs, and the moral values he
applies to assess the phenomena of dissolution in the bourgeois
family often seem inflexible and stuffy. In his zeal to denounce the
'immorality' of the bourgeoisie he erected an ideal of purity and
chastity which was the very one to which bourgeois patriarchalism
had paid homage and under which the woman was anything but
free. Thus he speaks of the 'licentiousness of sexual demands', of
the 'immorality and corruption which works its way like a creeping
poison through the body (of society)', of 'illegitimate male desires',
of the 'jungle-like satisfaction of the sexual impulse' and of the
'wildest orgies of the white slave-owners'.[29]

The very fact that Bebel gave the name of 'free love' to the
sexual relationship which he idealized shows particularly clearly
the break between his rigour and the ideal.

Bebel said that it was the task of the socialist movement to
re-establish, at the higher level of a socialist order of society, the
freedom of woman, which had been lost in the course of the
historical process through the rule of the male on the basis of
private property. From the suppression of women as a sexual being
he deduced her common cause with the proletariat, and from
socialism he expected her emancipation along with that of the
proletariat as a whole. Bebel's book became the most important
educational work during the period of the Party's persecution
particularly among women workers. 'For the proletarian woman
who was intellectually alive, Bebel was almost always the way to
Marx'.[30] Numerous personal testimonies, such as those of Rosa
Luxemburg, Clara Zetkin, Marie Juchacz, Ottilie Baader, and Luise
Zietz, give evidence of the enduring effect that Bebel's book had
on women.[31] It prepared the ground for the achievements of the
Social Democratic women's movement after 1890 in the realms of
education, agitation and organization.

Six years later (1884) Engels's work, *The Origin of the
Family, Private Property and the State*, was published. In this book,
Engels pursued Marx's uncompleted studies on the history of the
family using the latter's manuscripts and bringing them together
above all with the findings of L. H. Morgan, as published in his
Ancient Society in 1877. According to Engels, Morgan's research
basically modified Marx's views on the role of the family in economic development.[32]

With respect to the historical ethnological constructions on which Engels based his work, the same reservations apply as in the case of Bebel, who later likewise used data from Morgan. Engels was subsequently subjected to a radical critique from Marxist quarters. Both Cunow and Kautsky revised Engels on points where he had, in their opinion, introduced factors outside the system into the materialist causation. Cunow pointed out that Engels had distinguished a two fold character for the 'production and reproduction of immediate life'. In his preface to the book, Engels described this as follows:

> On the one side, the production of the means of existence, of food, clothing and shelter, and the tools necessary for that production; on the other side, the production of human beings themselves, the propagation of the species.

Cunow rejected the idea that the 'production of human beings' constituted an independent factor of development and argued that men's relationship to the female sex was dependent on women's economic position and the women's status was determined by their importance as 'labour power for the general livelihood'.[33] Naturally, Cunow's criticism was not intended to deny the importance of the sexual impulse. Rather, it sought to emphasize that the social form of the sexual relationship depended on the conditions of material production. The justice of Cunow's criticism is shown at those points where Engels tries to verify the hypothetical distinction he has made. He comes to the conclusion that the driving force behind the transition from polygamy to monogamy was the women's longing for 'chastity', for 'temporary or lasting marriage with a single man', or for 'deliverance'.[34] Kautsky, like Cunow, discarded forced constructions of this kind, which presupposed the psychology of the bourgeois age, and stressed in contrast the importance of the division of labour between the sexes in the formation of bourgeois pairing relationships.[35]

In the context of our theme Engels's theorem that as the accompaniment of the further development of private property women were enslaved and deprived of their social power, is also important. The situation had only been reversed in the most recent period through the re-introduction of women into the process of production. It would finally be superseded only in socialism.[36]

4/1889-1913

In 1889, Clara Zetkin attended the Paris International Workers' Congress, along with six other women, as a representative of the European organizations for women workers. At the conference, she specified and extended theoretically all the insights about women's emancipation that existed within Social Democracy at that time. She described female labour as the precondition for the emancipation of women. The Socialists were accused of sharing the reactionary view of those who sought to abolish female labour. The economic developments of the time, she claimed, made it necessary for women to work, and their work contributed to the tendency for every individual's working hours to be reduced and for social wealth to increase. Socialists ought to have known that:

> it is not female labour as such that lowers wages through competition with male labour, but the exploitation of women workers by the capitalist, who appropriates their labour. Above all, the Socialists ought to know that economic dependence or independence is the basis for social slavery or liberty . . . Just as the male worker is subjugated by the capitalist, so is the woman by the man, and she will always remain in subjugation until she is economically independent. Work is the indispensable condition for economic independence.[1]

Since female labour was thus an economic necessity and the only means of liberating women from sexual slavery, Clara Zetkin emphatically opposed any restrictions on it. She also spoke out against special protection for women workers: 'We demand no more protection than labour as a whole demands against capital.'[2] It was true, she said, that in their employment women would only swap one master for another, the husband for the employer. But they would at least gain their independence from their husbands and thereby be placed in the same position as all wage earners under capitalism.[3]

Although the Congress greeted Zetkin's speech with tumultuous applause, it resolved to demand a series of protective measures, namely the

> prohibition of female labour in all branches of industry where the work is particularly damaging to the female organism; the prohibition of night work for women and young workers under the age of 18; the prohibition of such branches of industry and labour processes as are prospectively detrimental to the health of the workers.
>
> The Congress further declares, that male workers have a duty to take women into their ranks on a basis of equal rights, and demands in principle: equal pay for equal work for the workers of both sexes and without distinctions as to nationality.[4]

It is conspicuous that the demand for the prohibition of branches of industry detrimental to health went further than the similar demand for the 'prohibition of female labour in all branches of industry where the work is particularly damaging to the female organism'.

The fact that the International Congress came out in favour of special protection for women was connected with the capitalist nature of the relations of production. Women offered themselves on the labour market at a lower price than men. Where employers were not prohibited legally from employing women in special cases, they had no reason to take on expensive male workers. This reinforced Zetkin's claim that 'the unwholesome consequences of female labour, which are so painfully felt today, will only disappear along with the capitalist process of production'.[5]

On the one hand, there was an urgent need to relieve the distress of the working-class families. Women had to be prohibited from doing particularly heavy and unhealthy jobs. On the other hand, it was also a good tactical ploy to put the primary emphasis on the protection of women and children. The greatest likelihood of success lay in demanding an improvement in social legislation for the weakest members of society, and this legislation could then be extended to the workers as a whole.

Seen from this angle, the Conference's demand for protection especially aimed at women appears as the minimum goal which could be realized, which was then to lead to the more far-reaching general protection of workers.

Chronologically speaking, protection for women workers was the first demand made by Social Democracy in the sphere of women's emancipation. It was already included in the Eisenach and Gotha Programs, and together with the right to work, the right to vote and civic and legal equality with the male it constituted the programme which the Social Democrats expected would, if realized, bring about the liberation of women, to the extent that this was possible at all in society as it then was. The demands for women's right to work, female suffrage and equal rights did not go beyond the framework of capitalist society, and simply sought to broaden civil rights which were not completely democratic into 'universal human rights' instead of 'male rights'. Such demands were made particularly by the bourgeois women's movements, but it was a different matter as far as protection for women workers was concerned. This was not only a formal legal measure, but implied interference with the employers' power of decision. For this reason it was precisely the socialist women's movement that demanded protection for women workers, while the bourgeois movement, in contrast, did not include it in the category of desirable reforms.

The bourgeois women's movement, in accordance with the way in which women's liberation developed in this class, had to strive in the first instance for completely free competition with men in the bourgeois occupations, that is, for the dismantlement of traditional male privileges. The women of the bourgeoisie could only gain their liberty by breaking out of the patriarchal family and rejecting decisively all the 'indulgence' with which the men had long treated them; they had to condemn any special provisions as such. At the time of the Paris Congress of Socialists even Clara Zetkin was still a declared opponent of any restrictions on female labour and of any special rights for women. It soon became evident, however, that this principle was untenable. Even if it was true that women could achieve their emancipation only if they were also exploited in a completely equal manner, it was also true that women were in a weaker position than men. They were forced to take work in defiance of socially sanctioned ideas of the woman's role, because the wages of the husbands or fathers of families were inadequate. But: 'Machinery, by throwing every member of that family on to the labour market, spreads the value of the man's labour power over his whole family.'[6] This enabled the employer to keep women's wages lower than men's. The wages of the married woman worker at least represented additional income, but the unmarried woman, who was completely dependent on her earnings, had to endure the wage level determined by the married woman, so that women came to have a depressing effect on men's wages, and married women on the wages of their unmarried fellow workers.

The separation between bourgeois and proletarian women did not only arise from the fact that the former wanted to abolish women's privileges, while the latter were fighting for special legislation to protect women workers. They also confronted one another as rivals on the labour market. As was shown by the Enquiry into the Situation of Women Workers which was initiated by the Reichstag in 1885, women from the middle and petty bourgeoisie, apart from their use as officials in the postal and educational services, found work in the lingerie and confectionery industries. They were employed predominantly in jobs which required 'care, cleanliness, taste, even art, and above all initiative'. Other than women proletarians and the 'widows and orphans of the lower class of public servants', there was a third category, consisting of the workers, for the productivity of labour was suffering through the

> women and daughters of still living public servants, whose salary was perfectly adequate for the essentials of life, but no longer provided enough for entertainment and better clothing for their daughters. Because they are not exposed to the same social misery as the women and girls of the working class . . . they force the wages and living conditions of their less well-placed rivals down to the very worst.[7]

In this situation, Clara Zetkin's original position, according to which women needed only such protection as was granted to all workers, was inadequate. For the wages and living conditions of women workers were far lower than the standard of their male counterparts. The male workers were better placed physically and socially. To make no special provisions for the protection of female labour under such circumstances was to agree to additional exploitation for the sake of an abstract notion of equality. Even before the organized work force was able to use its weapons to put pressure on the employers, the latter had decided to implement certain provisions for the protection of certain groups of workers, for the productivity of labour was suffering through the increasing misery, extensive exploitation had reached its absolute limit and the existence of society itself was threatened. Where capital recognized inequality in labour, however, the working-class movement could not possibly adhere dogmatically to a notion of equality.

Chronologically speaking, the protection of children took first place. The first law protecting children was introduced in England in 1819, in Prussia in 1839.[8] In the case of women, the only legal provisions for protection consisted of a three-week break after childbirth. In 1891, it became illegal to employ women in mining underground, their working day was restricted to 11 hours and the rest period after childbirth was extended to four weeks.[9] The Social Democrats held the view that the legislators had been brought to take these protective measures not out of any philanthropic intentions but because the sons of the working class were becoming increasingly unsuitable for military service.[10] The provisions for workers' protection by no means led to a reduction in profits. Rather, restrictions on the extensive volume of work (maximum hours of work) and the prohibition of certain jobs for women was compensated for by increasing the intensity of labour and the productivity of the workers.

Although even those who adhered unconditionally to the equality of the sexes finally came to endorse this scanty legislation, this no longer contradicted their ideal of equality. For, unlike in the early period of the German working-class movement, the emphasis lay not on the complete abolition of female labour, but on improving conditions of work. This presupposed that the organizations of the working class had found effective means of presenting their demands, instead of merely appealing to the ruling classes, and that economic development had advanced far enough for the employers to abandon their old methods of exploitation. When, in 1877, the Social Democratic caucus in the Reichstag introduced a bill to alter the industrial code, dealing thoroughly for the first time with the situation of women and making demands for protection,[11] the working-class movement did not have sufficient power to force through such a reform, and economic development had not advanced far enough in Germany. Protection for women was only improved in 1891. By this time Social Democracy had abandoned its senseless opposition to female labour as well as its insistence on the absolute equality of working conditions for both sexes under capitalism. A comprehensive programme for the protection of women workers was drawn up, which was continually adapted to the changing conditions of production and gradually turned into reality.

In 1889 Clara Zetkin published a pamphlet entitled *The Question of Women Workers and Women at the Present Time*. In it, she summarized all the notions of the state on the women question which had existed in German Social Democracy up to that time and assessed the works of Bebel and Engels. Because of its clarity and theoretical consistency, this brochure was both the most important product of the literature on women's emancipation and the guideline for the ensuing policy of Social Democracy on the woman question until the liquidation of the theory of women's emancipation in the Weimar period. Zetkin demonstrated that ever since the rule of matriarchal law, the female sex had been suppressed, and that women's situation corresponded to that of the productively occupied mass of the people. It was true, she said, that morality and religion had given this state of affairs the appearance of an eternal law, but it was nonetheless the outcome of conditions based on the relations of production of a given time. Restricted to the narrow confines of the home, women had been given the task of propagating the species and performing the services of domestic slaves. To the extent that the productive function of the family was eroded by the rise of industry, the basis of woman's economic influence within the family was destroyed. The women of the upper classes became objects of luxury, the women of the middle classes aspired to the liberal occupations, while those of the proletariat were driven into industry. By this process, however, the economic revolution not only annihilated the basis of the former family life, but also offered women the chance of emancipation.

Zetkin then went into the effects of female labour in industry, the pressure of women on men's wages, and the pressure of children on the wages of women. In her view, attempts to abolish female labour for this reason, however, were as hopeless as they were foolish, and were analogous to attempts to destroy machines. On the one hand, the economic facts could not be reversed. Capitalism could not do without female labour in industry. On the other, the abolition of female labour would once again return women to their former dependence on the husband. The only possible way of getting rid, not of female labour as such, but of the damage arising from its conditions under capitalism, was to socialize the means of production. Complete emancipation would only come with labour's emancipation from capital. The first essential step in this direction was to organize the industrial woman worker, to educate her politically and economically, and to bring her into solidarity with the men of her class. Even under capitalism, the increase of female labour was making society take over functions of the family. Only socialism, however, could guarantee that these functions were adequately performed. In the last resort, therefore, the complete emancipation of women proved to be an economic question, which was intimately connected with the question of the worker, and which could finally be solved only in conjunction with the latter.[12]

Clara Zetkin's pamphlet completed the socialist theory of women's emancipation. The further work of Social Democracy consisted, in the theoretical sphere, in specifying subordinate questions and, in the political sphere, in translating Zetkin's principles into the practical work of agitation among women workers and enlisting them in organizations. This task, again under the active guidance of Clara Zetkin, was dealt with in the following 25 years before the outbreak of the First World War.

At the Halle Party Conference, in 1890, Emma Ihrer reported on the preparations for the publication of a women's paper. As early as 1884, the Duchess Guilleaume-Schack, a convert to Social Democracy, had begun publishing *Die Staatsbürgerin* (*The Woman Citizen*) in Offenbach.[13] Towards the end of 1890, the first issue of *Die Arbeiterin* (*The Woman Worker*) appeared in Hamburg: the paper soon got into financial difficulties, however. At the Party Conference, Emma Ihrer stressed the 'seriousness' of the women's endeavours:

> We are not after a special movement for women, a game; we only want to support the general working-class movement, but then we also count on your support. We have a right to be treated by you as comrades with full rights. If you give us your material and intellectual support, it will bear fruit. It is not a question of a game, but of the total seriousness of our times.[14]

Emma Ihrer's speech was a mixture of justification for the women's movement, a plea for recognition and an appeal to historical inevitability.

The women proposed two resolutions in Halle. One called for the appointment of female factory inspectors, which the Socialist caucus had already demanded in the Reichstag in 1884,[15] and the other for the prohibition of health-damaging work for men and women. In the discussion on the resolutions, which completely followed Zetkin's line of equal protection for men and women and the rejection of privileges for women, Oertel said:

> Female labour is only a part of the wider social question, and cannot be solved on its own by any means. As little as we men can succeed in winning a more human existence within contemporary society, just so little would the women succeed in obtaining those rights that belong to them by nature.[16]

Here, as at subsequent party conferences, the women's speeches were attentively received; the men had the impression, however, that the women were too querulous, did not achieve enough, and did not regard the progress of their cause sufficiently in relation to the general development of the working-class movement.

The Party conference in Halle basked in the light of the abolition of the Anti-Socialist Law and an electoral success which had given the Social Democrats 20 per cent of all the votes cast and 35 seats in the Reichstag.

> According to approximate statistics, 1,300 periodical or non-periodical publications and 332 workers' organizations had been prohibited under the Anti-Socialist Law. There had been 900 deportations, and 1,000 years of imprisonment had been imposed on 1,500 people.[17]

In her assessment of the period of persecution, Emma Ihrer said:

> The movement did not dwindle away for this reason, but grew in breadth and depth, and we owe this quite particularly to the combined endeavours of Messrs Puttkammer, Brausewetter and Köller, whose systematic chicaneries have brought the women workers' movement to full bloom. For every meeting that was banned or broken up, each new condemnation or closure of an association, has led not only individuals, but innumerable women to think again about law and justice, and that is the best way to bring women to class consciousness. It is the signpost to Social Democracy.[18]

In the period of persecution from 1878 to 1890:

> The working women, wives and daughters of Social Democrats experienced at first hand and at the hand of their children what it means to be a Social Democrat, and not just for the short duration

of a strike, but for years. . . . The secrecy with ˉwhich everything had to be done suddenly gave Marxism, with its complex
conceptual structure, a somewhat religious aura. The male and
female sides of the movement for workers' emancipation only
really got to know each other for the first time, and became
brothers and sisters through the 'community of defeat'.[19]

As is shown by the wealth of literature on organizations of
women workers, it was they which were particularly severely
affected by the persecution.[20] The number of organizations that
were re-established after the Law was abolished, however, showed
the ineffectiveness of the police endeavours. The increasing strength
of women's position in the workers' movement was also shown
by the fact that the General Commission of Trade Unions, set
up in 1890, took a woman on to its executive.

At the next Party Conference, in Erfurt in 1891, the Social
Democrats for the first time included in their programme the
express demand for 'universal, equal and direct suffrage, with
secret ballot, for all citizens of the Reich over twenty years of
age without distinction as to sex.' The 'Erfurt Programme' also
demanded

> the abolition of all laws which discriminate against women as
> compared with men in the public or private legal sphere, free educa-
> tion, free educational materials, and free care for those girls and
> boys who, because of their abilities, are considered suitable for
> further education.[21]

The Erfurt Programme did not contain any special provisions
for the protection of women. On this subject, however, Eduard
Bernstein made some fundamental comments in *Die Neue Zeit*:

> It is wrong to cry 'No workers' protection for women, which is not
> also given to men'. That is taken from the bourgeois twaddle about
> women's rights. It contradicts what we as socialists know. The
> woman worker, who is socially in a weaker position, has need of
> more energetic social protection than the man. She especially
> needs it in cases, such as domestic industry, where her particular
> social status is the cause of special abuses, of greater suppression.
> She further needs it in her role as the agent of the coming genera-
> tion, the one who gives birth. In any circumstances, equality stops
> at this point, for the woman fulfils a special sexual function, and
> with regard to this she has a claim to special protection by society.
> If the prohibition of work for women who have just given birth
> discriminates against them economically, then there is a simple

remedy: society should pay compensation . . . All these things do not constitute exceptional laws against women; they are merely an acknowledgement of actual differences. . . . To deduce legal distinctions from such differences is bourgeois ideology, and this may explain the confusion of bourgeois notions of women's rights.[22]

Two years later, Clara Zetkin published an article of the same tendency in *Die Gleichheit*.[23]

The Erfurt Conference resolved to set up special local 'agitation commissions' for women. These were to be loose organizations, to give a lead in agitation and correspondence and to arrange for the calling of meetings.

Female delegates at the International Workers' Congress in Brussels in 1891 asked the Congress 'to give definite expression in the Programme to the efforts towards equal rights for both sexes' and to demand, as a first step, that equal rights be granted in the areas of civil law and politics.[24] The opinion of one speaker in the discussion, that 'the primary duty of the woman was to live for her home', drew a vehement protest, whereupon the women's resolution was passed with only three votes against.[25]

The Party's Organizational Statutes passed in Halle in 1890 gave women the right, 'insofar as there are no women among the elected representatives of a constituency, to elect female delegates to Party conferences at special women's meetings'.[26] This privilege was abolished at the Berlin Party Conference at the instigation of Ottilie Baader, on the grounds that it was unfounded, but was reintroduced in Frankfurt am Main in 1894.[27] It also found its place in the Organizational Statutes adopted in Mainz in 1900.[28]

The Berlin Party Conference of 1892 set up a system of *Vertrauenspersonen** for women. At the request of the women Social Democrats from Mannheim, constitutional provision was made in the Party's Organizational Statutes for the election of permanent women's representatives, by replacing the term *Vertrauensmänner with Vertrauenspersonen*.[29] Although the Combination Laws forbade women to belong to political organizations, they did not affect the activity of individual persons, so that they could be circumvented by the network of *Vertrauenspersonen*. The

* The word *Vertrauensmann* means 'spokesman', and is also used as the German equivalent for 'shop steward'. It is a masculine word, however, and only by changing it to *Vertrauenspersonen* ('spokespeople') could it be used for both men and women. I have left it in the German throughout to make this distinction clear.—*Translator*

task of these representatives was described as 'educating proletarian women in political and trade-union matters' and awakening and reinforcing their class consciousness.[30] After the agitation commissions, which had been opened to women by a decision of the Party Conference in 1892, were banned in 1895, the system of *Vertrauenspersonen* obtained special significance for the political education and organization of women. Between 1901 and 1907 the number of female *Vertrauenspersonen* rose from 25 to 407. Their addresses were regularly published in *Die Gleichheit*. The Combination Laws, which were generally reactionary and particularly hostile to women, were abolished in 1908, and women joined the Party as regular members in accordance with the constitution for associations laid down as early as 1905 by the Jena Party Conference. A women's representative was now given a place on the Party's executive. The 'Central Bureau for Women Comrades', which was led by two women with equal powers, remained in existence until 1917.[31]

In 1891 the first issue of the Social Democratic women's magazine, *Die Gleichheit (Equality)*, appeared in Stuttgart as the successor to *Die Arbeiterin*. It carried the sub-title, 'For the Interests of the Woman Worker', and was edited by Emma Ihrer, with Clara Zetkin taking the responsibility for the contents. When *Die Gleichheit* failed to strengthen the ranks of Social Democratic women, criticism of the editorial staff was voiced within the Party. A resolution was proposed at the Gotha Party Conference in 1896, demanding 'a women's paper which was thoroughly intelligible to all' and which should appear as a Sunday supplement to the Party papers.[32] The resolution did not get sufficient support. In 1898, the Stuttgart Party Conference rejected the suggestion that the ownership of *Die Gleichheit* be transferred to the Party and the editorship be moved to Berlin. In reply to accusations that *Die Gleichheit* had failed to produce a large movement of women workers, Clara Zetkin said that this was the task of agitation and organization. *Die Gleichheit*, she said, could only do one thing, and that was 'to provide an educational and promotional influence within the movement', and this it had done. *Die Gleichheit* has pursued one principal goal, which was to put the women comrades who were in the forefront of the struggle firmly on the ground of Social Democracy.'[33]

Time and again there were attempts to adapt *Die Gleichheit* to the alleged wishes of the 'broad membership' and to give it a 'popular' form. Such attacks on the theoretical level of her magazine were continually refuted by Clara Zetkin. The job of *Die Gleichheit* was not at all to win new members. Rather, it existed for the 'more advanced women comrades'. Recruitment of members had to be achieved by pamphlets and organizational spade-work. The quality of the magazine ought not to be sacrificed to some alleged mass attraction.[34] Even in the period of its widest distribution (from 1900 to 1913 the circulation increased from 4,000 to 112,000) *Die Gleichheit* had to endure attacks. Most of the accusation concerned the fact that the magazine was 'difficult to understand'.[35] If such attacks are compared with those on the official theoretical organ of the Party, *Die Neue Zeit*, which were of a similar tenor, then it is easy to see that talk of it being 'difficult to understand' was really only a pretext for the rejection of the Marxist views put forward by these magazines. As revisionist tendencies gained in importance within the Party, there were first changes of personnel on the editorial boards, and then finally *Die Neue Zeit* folded completely in 1922, followed by *Die Gleichheit* in the following year.

The attitude of the Social Democrats towards the protection of women again came up for discussion at the next International Workers' Congress in Zürich in 1893. Luise Kautsky, the wife of the author of the Erfurt Programme, gave the report on this question, after which she proposed the following resolution:

> In view of the fact that the bourgeois women's movement rejects any special legislation to provide legal protection for women workers on the grounds that it interferes with women's freedom and her equal rights with the male; and that, therefore, this movement does not, on the one hand, take into account the nature of contemporary society, which is based on the exploitation of the working class—women as well as men—by the capitalist class; and that it fails on the other, to recognize that through the differentiation of the sexes woman obtains a special role, namely as the mother of the children, which is so important for the future of society; the Zürich International Congress declares that it is the duty of the representatives of women workers from all countries to advocate most emphatically legal protection for women workers.

Demands for the protection of women workers were then drawn up in seven points.[36]

Luise Kautsky departed from Zetkin's line in her speech, for she described female labour as the 'battering ram for the protection of men' and claimed that women were not making demands for their own sakes, but that it was all done 'to promote the interests of society as a whole'. It was of course true that women's protection put restrictions on the exploitation of women workers and thus indirectly brought an improvement for all the workers. Instead of expressing this historical inevitability, however, which had its roots in women's large share in the work-force, she delivered a statement in which the women apologized for their demands for protection, saying that until that time they had been the 'battering ram for the protection of men' and that the demands for the 'protection of women' were put forward 'not in the interests of their own sex, but to promote the interests of society as a whole'. The fact that the protection of women workers would diminish women's distress was obviously an insufficient justification. Obeisance had still to be made to the men, and the 'interests of society as a whole' had to be brought in to give the necessary emphasis to protection for women. This declaration did not exactly testify to the independent consciousness of the women's movement or to a correct assessment of its importance by the Party as a whole.

The discussion which developed on the relationship between the woman question and prostitution was very characteristic of the basic attitude towards it as well as the limitations of this attitude. It was an old Social Democratic principle that the prohibition or wide-scale restriction of female labour would drive the women excluded from production in this manner into prostitution as the only way of earning their own living. Both Marx and Bebel gave statistical evidence of a connexion between falling wages for women workers and increasing prostitution.[37] The same facts were applied to Kautsky's resolution by a Dutch woman. Zetkin, it is true, said in reply that protected women workers were much less likely to lapse into prostitution than those who had no protection.

There is no doubt an element of truth in both views. If women were excluded from certain jobs, the question arose as to how they could earn their livelihood if the demand was insufficient in jobs remaining open to them. The gap was meant to be filled by the higher wages paid to the men who took over the women's jobs. This wage rise, however, only benefited the women who lived in a family, not those who were on their own. For the first category, the husbands' higher income reduced the constraint to take work, so that possibly the female demand for jobs, to some extent reduced, could be satisfied within the 'open occupations'. According to this theory, women would easily find work in periods of full employment. This does not solve the question, however, as to whether a slump in the economy would not cause the employers primarily to lay off the 'protected women', since they were relatively expensive labour power. The advantage of lower wages for women, which actually made them more desirable than men as labour power, would then be abolished by their protection in times of crisis. In the first years of the Weimar Republic, however, it was shown that it was not the employers, but the employed men, who forced women to be dismissed, either by the direct means of co-determination in the factory, or indirectly by the regulation of the labour market carried out in their interest. Protection for women was effective only in periods of economic prosperity.

The Cologne Party Conference of 1893 passed on a resolution proposing the appointment of female factory inspectors to the Social Democratic caucus in the Reichstag (who introduced it there in 1894) and rejected two further resolutions without discussion. The first of these pointed to the increase in female labour, and the other to the consequent need for agitation both among the female proletariat and in the family, 'so that the following generation, of both sexes, naturally, may, by being schooled in this way, help to realize the cause of the whole world's proletariat'.[38] The reason for the rejection of the resolutions, which seems incomprehensible in view of the Party theory's friendly attitude to women, ought perhaps to be sought in the fact that the requested consideration of female labour had already been given a place in the Party Programme and in the women's movement.

In 1894, the Social Democrats introduced a bill for women's suffrage in the Reichstag, but it was rejected by the majority. As reason for their resolution, they pointed to the injustice of excluding women from political rights and to the need, in view of their distressed position, to give them representation in the legislative bodies.[39] It is worthy of note that in this case, in a parliamentary context there was a transition from the demand for female suffrage as a weapon in the class struggle to a more formally democratic argument.

At the Breslau Party Conference of 1895, the women proposed a further resolution which was passed on to the parliamentary party: it demanded that all clauses discriminating against women should be removed from the draft code of civil law, and that unmarried women and their children be given equal rights. The Breslau Conference also adopted a resolution which demanded that a centre be set up to gather material on the situation of women workers in individual branches of industry and obliged the Party to publish special cases. The Party further decided to broaden their demand for workers' protection to include domestic industry. Women in particular were affected by this. The 'male comrades' were also called on once again to help overcome the backwardness of the women.[40]

The International Congress of Socialist Workers and Trade Unions, held in London in 1896, renewed the obligation on trade unions to accept working women as members and to demand equal pay for equal work by men and women, and placed on society the responsibility for supporting women in the post-natal period for the duration of their absence from work.[41]

After Paris (1889) and Erfurt (1891), the most important step in the evolution of the Social Democratic theory of women's emancipation was taken by the Party Conference at Gotha in 1896. Clara Zetkin presented the report on the woman question, which followed the lines of her 1889 brochure. The question was put in completely different terms for the grand bourgeoisie, the middle and petty bourgeoisie and the proletariat, in accordance with the class position of each. From this distinction she derived the incompatibility of the bourgeois and proletarian women's movement. The most important distinguishing feature, she stressed, was the fact that the bourgeois women's movement was waging a struggle against the men of its own class, while the women proletarians were fighting, in conjunction with the men of their class, for the abolition of the rule of capital. It was decided by a majority vote to print Zetkin's speech in the form of a pamphlet.[42] The Party Conference adopted a lengthy resolution on the woman question,[43] which took up the major points of Zetkin's speech, but was unclear in a number of respects. It maintained, for example, that the women of the upper class were fighting 'to remove all social distinctions based on the ownership of income'. Clara Zetkin, in contrast, had explained that these women were endeavouring to get disposal over the income brought in to them in their marriage, which until then had been administered by the husband. Their 'struggle' was thus by no means aimed at the removal of all social distinctions based on the ownership of income, but against the male's exclusive power of disposal over this income. Furthermore, precisely such 'inactivity' on women's part stood in contradiction to the independence claimed by upper-class women from the man as the 'owner of income'. Such independence ought to be achieved first.

Also, the statement that the emancipatory struggle of women workers was not a struggle against the men of their own class, but in conjunction with them, was only true to the extent that they belonged to a common class. Even the organization of women workers could not resolve the antagonism which arose between male and female workers on the labour market, however, quite apart from the fact that women workers generally proved somewhat inaccessible to political education and recruitment into trade unions.

The Party Conference further passed an 8-point programme to improve the situation of women. It demanded: the extension of protection for women workers, active and passive voting rights for the industrial courts, equal political rights, equal education and freedom of occupation for both sexes, equal status in private law, the abolition of the system of servants in order to liberate the domestics, and equal pay for equal work. The demand for equal pay for equal work by men and women was first raised in 1865. Employers later used the argument that women were less efficient than men to refuse this demand, but the argument was inapplicable to equal work. For the demand for equal wages referred precisely to the fact that women were paid less than men even when they produced just as much in just the same time. Such a case clearly shows that the level of wages is not determined by the use-value of labour to the employer, that is to say, by the value imparted to the product of work in the course of the working day, but that it is in fact determined by the exchange-value of this labour to the worker, that is, by what it costs him to maintain his ability to work. The exchange-value of female labour, however, was lower than that of the male. Hence if men and women did the same amount of work in the same length of time, the fact that women were paid less meant that more surplus value was obtained from them. As long as the employer could in this way find cheap labour, he had no cause to concede the demand for equal wages. For this reason, only trade-union pressure could bring women's wages up to par with men's.

The situation was no different in jobs where there was no immediately equivalent male labour to act as a standard of measure, that is to say, in occupations and factories where the men and women were engaged in different types of work. Here we either have another case of simple labour, so that despite the fact that men and women perform different jobs the two can very well be compared—or there is a genuine distinction between male and female labour as higher and simple labour. Disregarding the case in which the higher labour of a woman is worse paid than the simple labour of a man, there is certainly a tendency for women to be used for simple labour. This is due both to the genuine backwardness of the women and their fear of competition. Female labour in this sphere cannot be said to be less efficient, however, since men traditionally do not perform such activities, and as a result of their special qualifications (skill, speed, etc) the women, comparatively speaking, are more productive than the men.

Whether the allegation that women are less efficient is automatically refuted by the equal productivity of their work where the personnel is mixed, or whether it is a question of expressly female occupations being underpaid, or whether there is a distinction between simple and higher labour, in each case lower wages for women can be explained by the historical situation of the women workers. This state of affairs can only be altered through trade-union struggle. An important point in the discussion of women's wages is the contradiction between the demand for equal pay, which presupposes equal work, and the demand for women's protection, which makes allowance for their lower efficiency. Gertrude Hanna, the women's secretary of the trade unions, suggested that the notion of 'equivalent efficiency' be introduced to resolve this contradiction.[44] This was to enable comparisons to be made between different categories of male and female labour.

The precondition for any comparison between male and female labour, as between different types of labour as a whole, is the establishment of an objective standard of measure for the use-value of labour. Modern wage agreements provide such a standard by setting up job categories in which characteristics of labour (ability, responsibility, efficiency and environmental factors) are brought together in a series of rising demands. The wage groups are based on the job categories. The workers are grouped together according to the principle that their particular form of work qualification corresponds to a particular use-value for the employer. Equal payment is demanded for equal use-value. The employers endeavoured to maintain the inequality of women's wages despite objective assessment of their job characteristics by giving women less than the equivalent male pay scale, or by setting up special female groups which were separate from the normal assessment schemes.

Only recently, since rights for women have also been made mandatory in wage agreements, has the category of 'women's wages' disappeared from such agreements; it is now also impermissible to make contractual deductions from women's wages as based on their place in the scale. Admittedly, trade unions had already previously succeeded in bringing women's wages close to those of men. But only when special wage groups for women workers were abolished was the precondition created for remuneration on the basis, not of the sex of the worker, but of the use-value of his or her work. This did not mean the end of the discussion on equal pay, however. The object of the struggle is now the place on the scale itself. The fact that female labour has traditionally been underestimated and that it is to the employer's advantage to underpay women workers means that pressure is applied in the categorization of women. All the measures aimed at putting pressure on their wages derive from the fact that women's share in poorly paid jobs is greater than that of men.

In line with this, every attempt is made, with the aid of work assessment, to arrange the differences between lower and upper wage categories in such a way that women are as far as possible put into the lower groups. In cases where the workforce is mixed, the better paid men can be withdrawn from the production process in order to get around an increase in women's wages. In analogy to the effect of the previous contractual wage-reductions for women, the job characteristics in enterprises mainly employing women can be chosen in such a way that the women never get beyond the lower wage levels, by which means the discriminatory category of women's wages is re-introduced. To the extent that in a general sense it is no longer legally permissible to pay women less, work assessment does of course represent a step forward in the question of equal rights. The social responsibility to compensate women for absence from work for reasons of childbirth and post-natal rest has also been recognized. The contradiction between protection for women workers and equal pay has been abolished. However, both with respect to their placement in the scale, and with respect to their wage-level in general, women are dependent now as before on the emphatic representation of their interests by the working-class movement.[45]

Table 1

Survey of Socialist organization among women up to 1913.[46]

Year	No of female workers	female trade union members	per cent	female SPD members	circulation of Die Gleichheit	Female Party Delegates	Female Vertrauens-Personen
1875	1,116,695[a]						
1882	5,541,517[b]						
1890						4[k]	
1891		4,355[c]	1.8[c]			6[l]	
1894		5,251[c]	2.1[c]				
1895	6,578,350[b]	6,697[c]	2.5[c]			7[m]	
1896		15,295[c]	4.6[c]				
1898		13,009[c]	2.7[c]			6[n]	
1899		19,280[c]	3.3[c]			5[o]	
1900		22,844[c]	3.3[c]		c. 4,000		
1901		23,699[c]	3.4[c]				25[v]
1902		28,218[c]	3.8[c]				54[v]
1903		40,666[c]	4.5[c]		9,500[h]		78[v]
1904		48,604[c]	4.6[c]		12,000[h]		100[v]
1905		74,441[c]	5.7[c]	4,000[e]	23,000[e]		190[v]
1906		118,908[c]	7.1[c]	6,460[e]	46,000[e]	29[p]	325[v]
1907	9,492,881[b]	136,929[c]	7.3[c]	10,943[f]	70,000[i]	16[i]	407[v]
1908		138,443[c]	7.6[c]	29,458[f]		32[q]	
1909				62,259[f]	77,000[f]	17[r]	
1910		189,442[d]		82,642[g]	82,000[j]	20[j]	
1911				107,693[g]	94,000[g]	36[s]	
1912				130,371[g]	107,000[g]	35[t]	
1913				141,115[g]	112,000[g]	29[u]	

The jumps in the readership of *Die Gleichheit* coincided with a marked increase in the number of female *Vertrauenspersonen* and in female membership in the Party and trade unions. In 1882, the number of working women stood at 4,259,103, or 18.5 per cent of the total work force. By 1895 it had risen to 5,264,393, or 20 per cent, and in 1907 it reached 8,243,498 or 26.4 per cent of all workers.[47]

The 44.3 per cent increase in the number of working women in the period from 1895 to 1907 contrasted with a 2,000 per cent increase in female membership in the trade unions, while subscriptions to *Die Gleichheit* rose by only 152 per cent.

The phenomenal growth in the strength of the women's movement in the period 1900-1913 was due primarily to the increase in the number of women workers, and secondly to the expiry of the old Combination Law and the agitation of the Social Democrats, which skilfully exploited the domestic and foreign situation (the colonial question, the growth of the military budget, the build-up of the fleet, and rising food prices).

A study of the distribution of articles on questions concerning women in *Die Neue Zeit*, the official theoretical paper of the Social Democratic Party, from 1883 to 1923 likewise reveals that most of the articles devoted to the woman question were written in the years 1989–1912. Of the total of 498 articles, including notices and book reviews, 229, or 46.9 per cent, appeared in these fifteen years, so that almost half of the total were published in about one third of the period. In this shorter period, 36.4 per cent of the total number of articles were published, hence a third of the total in a quarter of all the years of publication. The 498 articles fit into 13 categories:

1   The greatest number of contributions, totalling 98, were reviews of a great variety of books on questions concerning women. These were followed by:
2   55 articles on morality, prostitution and sexual diseases.
3   47 articles on biological-social relations (including marriage, divorce, the ratio between the sexes, and the decline in the birth-rate).
4   46 articles on women in various occupations (monographs, enquiries, statistics).
5   35 general articles on female labour.
6   35 general articles on the educational system.
7   33 articles on literary topics (analyses, reviews, etc).
8   33 articles on ethnological research on marriage and the family.
9   29 articles on women in politics, the Party and the trade unions.
10   23 articles on women's legal status.
11   22 general articles of a programmatic nature on the emancipation of women.
12   21 biographies, obituaries and assessments of famous women.
13   14 articles on women's emancipation in other countries.

Apart from this, the Supplement published 21 stories, in 140

instalments (by, among others, Arno Holz, Minna Kautsky, Elisa-
beth Langer, the Goncourt brothers, Marcel Prévost, René Bazin,
Maupassant, Chekhov, and Gorki), which dealt in literary form
with questions of concern to women. If we disregard the book
reviews, the interest of *Die Neue Zeit* was concentrated primarily
on the sexual relations of the working class, followed in second
and third place by articles on demographic phenomena and female
labour. These three thematic groups, which were concerned with
the material basis for women's emancipation, correspond to categories 6 to 13, which describe women's position in the social super-
structure and the goals and advances of the revolutionary women's
movement. This arrangement shows that the analysis of questions
connected with women's liberation was orientated on the theory
of scientific socialism, although the pre-eminence of sexuality does
not fit in with this. The increasingly influential *Sozialistische
Monatshefte (Socialist Monthly)*, the most important publication
after the official *Neue Zeit*, reveals a similar picture as regards the
chronological distribution of articles on questions concerning
women. In this magazine too, most of the contributions on women's
emancipation are found in the period 1902–1913. It is true that
the highest total for one year did not come until 1917, with the
multiplication of contributions on the problems of female labour
during the war, but before and after this one year a downward
tendency predominated. The *Sozialistische Monatshefte* devoted the
greatest amount of space to articles on general questions of women's
emancipation (for example, the psychology of the sexes, the future
of marriage, free love, and marriage and one's career). These
were followed by contributions on the women's movement, female
labour, the legal status of women, socio-hygienic and socio-ethical
questions, biographies, women in politics and book reviews.

A comparison between the Marxist *Neue Zeit* and the reformist *Sozialistische Monatshefte* reveals, initially, that the frequency of articles on women questions was different in the two
periodicals. In the forty years 1883 to 1922, the number of
articles appertaining to this theme in *Die Neue Zeit* was greater
in absolute terms than that in the 35 volumes of the *Sozialistische
Monatshefte*. There were in fact about four times as many contributions in *Die Neue Zeit* as in the *Sozialistische Monatshefte*.

Whereas the emphasis in *Die Neue Zeit* lay on research into
the conditions governing life and work of women, the *Sozialistische
Monatshefte* tended in the main to publish general reflections on

the scope, nature and limits of the women's movement and to provide relatively little concrete material on the real situation of women workers. The final years of the war, when most of the articles on female labour appeared, were an exception, but this was due to the increase in female labour at that time and the discussion sparked off by Edmund Fischer on the relationship between socialism and the woman question, particularly female labour. *Die Neue Zeit* presented the women's movement as a necessary process and studied its progress, its contradictions and its possible completion through socialism. The *Sozialistische Monatshefte* in contrast, devoted its attention, on the one hand, to questions of the organization of the women's movement and, on the other, to philosophical and psychological reflections on the nature of woman and her emancipation. A great deal was written about the woman of the future. There were also, admittedly, some contributions on the occupational, legal and political situation of women, but the overthrow of the capitalist relations of production was by no means regarded as the central problem of women's liberation. The characteristic feature of the *Sozialistische Monatshefte* was rather that it gave concrete presentations of working conditions in individual female occupations, the question of women's suffrage, social security for mothers, widows and orphans, the proceedings of women's conferences, and women's participation in political and trade-union affairs. The wealth of material presented, however, was not suitably interpreted in the theoretical articles, which were in fact peculiarly non-committal. The material conditions and social situation of women were not, as in *Die Neue Zeit*, explained by theory to be results of the capitalist economic system, but registered as facts, to which vague speculations about the 'problems of women's life, were counterposed without any connexion.

The most important new contribution to Social Democratic literature on the emancipation of women following the works by Bebel (1878) and Engels (1884) and Clara Zetkin's summary of the socialist theory of women's emancipation (1889) was Lilly Braun's book, *Die Frauenfrage* (*The Women's Question*) published in 1901. The book dealt with the development of the woman question up to the 19th century and the economic aspect of the problem in the modern period. It was based on an extensive study of source material and concurred, on the whole, with the Party theory.

The reception of Lilly Braun's book in Social Democracy was not as enduring as that of earlier works on the same theme. This was related, on the one hand, to its price and scope, on the other to the tendencies connected with her name within the Party. Bebel welcomed the new publication in a review in *Die Neue Zeit*, praised the author's diligence, specialized knowledge and style, criticized only her over-favourable assessment of Christianity as regards its effects on the status of women and her cursory treatment of the proletarian women's movement.[48] Lilly Braun, who came from a noble officer's family, was married to the writer Dr Heinrich Braun. The participation of both in *Die Zukunft*, edited by Maximilian Harden, was brought up in the controversy that took place at the Dresden Party Conference in 1903.[49] From the very start, no love was lost between Clara Zetkin and Lilly Braun. In *Die Gleichheit*, Clara Zetkin was only prepared to give her responsibility for the news section, and Kautsky rejected one of her articles for publication in *Die Neue Zeit*.[50] Within the Party both she and her husband sided with the Revisionists. After many controversies, the columns of *Die Gleichheit* were closed to her 'from about 1906', and the same happened in the case of most of the dailies as well.[51] Within the women's movement she particularly advocated maternity benefits, and co-operation with bourgeois women in the establishment of household cooperatives.[52]

The Social Democratic women of Germany held their first conference in Mainz in September 1900. On the agenda was the extension of the system of *Vertrauenspersonen*, agitation among women workers and the attitude to be taken by proletarian women to their bourgeois counterparts. From several resolutions it became obvious that a minority was seeking to depoliticize the women's movement and to get *Die Gleichheit* to deal with more 'popular' women's questions. Clara Zetkin, Ottillie Baader and Markwald opposed these resolutions on the grounds that the more advanced women comrades could not do without *Die Gleichheit*. If the magazine changed its character it would lose its significance without, however, getting through to the masses of women. In the first issue of the 11th volume of *Die Gleichheit* (1901), Clara Zetkin published her basic standpoint on the criticisms. She wrote that *Die Gleichheit* would, as previously,

> fight with all its energy and bite for the total liberation of the world of proletarian women, for the latter is only possible in a socialist society. Only in such a society, with the disappearance of the currently dominant economic and property relations, will the social opposition disappear between the haves and the have-

nots, between man and woman, and between intellectual and physical work. The abolition of such oppositions, however, can only come through class struggle: the liberation of the proletariat can only be the work of the proletariat itself. If the proletarian woman wants to be free, she must join forces with the general socialist movement. . . . The characteristic standpoint, that of class struggle, must be keenly and unambiguously stressed in a magazine for the interests of proletarian women. This must be done all the more keenly, moreover, the more the bourgeois women's libbers make it their business, by the use of general humanitarian phrases and petty concessions to the women workers' demands for reform, to bring intrigue into the world of proletarian women and to seek to draw them away from class struggle. Education of proletarian women precisely for the class struggle, however, will also in future be the chief task of *Die Gleichheit*.

The Women's Educational Associations were also attacked at the Mainz Conference on the grounds that they constantly turned into 'associations for gossip and bickering', because of the great poverty, lack of time and intellectual bondage of women. This radical position, it is true, obtained the support of only a weak majority, but in view of what happened after 1918 it is nonetheless remarkable that the will to retain women within the proletariat class struggle triumphed at all. The special nature of the methods of agitation and organization of women were to be stopped at the point where they disturbed the unity of the working-class movement.[53] In Mainz, Ottilie Baader was elected as the 'central *Vertrauensperson* for the women comrades of Germany'.

Protection for women workers, the women's movement, protection for children, and women's suffrage constantly recurred as the themes at subsequent women's conferences. The Women's Conference held before the Munich Party Conference of 1902 dealt with the training of women agitators, legal protection for female and child workers and domestic labour, and political equal rights for women, particularly with respect to freedom of association. In its report to the Party Conference that followed, the Party executive referred to the banning of numerous meetings because women were participating.[54]

Of greater importance to women was the Mannheim Conference, held in 1904. In her report to this conference, Ottilie Baader wrote:

The band of our followers has grown incessantly. Apart from

general educational agitation to spread the socialist viewpoint, the proletarian women's movement has exploited public events, characteristic of our times, to convince women of the need to participate in the struggles of their class. . . . Agitation against militarism, the law clericalizing the schools, the question of schools and education, the discussion on youth and socialism in *Die Gleichheit*, child labour

were, according to her, the most important topics of political educational work among women.[55]

The women's conference adopted a resolution on the subject of female suffrage, which said:

The demand for women's suffrage results from the economic and social revolutions provoked by the capitalist mode of production, but in particular from the revolutionary change in labour and the status and consciousness of women. By its very nature it is a consequence of the principle of bourgeois democracy which demands the removal of all social distinctions not based on property and proclaims completely equal legal rights for all adults in both private and public life as a right of personality.[56]

The argument had not changed since the Unification Party Conference at Gotha in 1875, but the accent had shifted. Previously, the justification of the suffrage by the principle of bourgeois democracy had been subordinate to the idea that universal suffrage would, since the great majority of voters would consist of workers, lead to the rule of the working class and to all the revolutionary changes connected with it.[57] In its present form, however, the justification of the suffrage remained completely within the concepts of the bourgeois view of the state.

Where previously one had proclaimed the right to work, now the working women's right to maternity leave was propagated. It was to be shown later that the different stress was to a certain extent connected with the economic situation. If the majority of women had jobs, the emphasis was placed on the protection of maternity, while in times of crisis, in contrast, it lay on the protection of women's right to work.

The shift in emphasis from agitation to make women conscious of their oppression, and hence from the advocacy of a 'theory of equal rights', to concern with concrete every-day political questions typified the change in the political climate and was undoubtedly both a cause and a symptom of the response to the socialist women's movement in this period. A closer definition of 'women's interests in politics' occurred, and women were made aware of the need to participate in questions of national and international politics. Themes such as 'freedom of association, protection for women workers, labour insurance, a statutory 8-hour day, the extension of industrial inspection, insurance against sickness, accidents, disablement and the death of a husband or father, customs and taxation policies, militarism and marinism', now dealt with as problems of agitation among women, testify to the fact that women's liberation was no longer grasped theoretically at the roots, but had become a question of awakening women's interests in current political struggles and showing them how politics 'affected them'. By this means it was sought to enable women to actually practice a kind of equality.[58] In the 1903 Reichstag election, for example, numerous 'women's electoral associations' were set up in Prussia. With the motto 'If we can't vote, we can still stir', the Social Democratic women took the election campaign into the factories, worker's apartment blocks and shops.[59]

This kind of agitation, however, also had its negative side. For the purposes of political mobilization it was necessary to concentrate on generally visible abuses which caused particular suffering to proletarian women, but this meant that opposition to the ruling system became fixed on certain concepts, above all in the sphere of social policy, and that the achievement of such goals took the place of the socialist transformation of society. The fatal dialectic of rise and decline triumphed here just as it had in the case of legislation for workers' protection in the working-class movement. The women's movement was unable, just like the working-class movement as a whole, to cling to the mere negation of existing social conditions. Rather, it had to get beyond asserting that women's emancipation was impossible under capitalism and make concrete suggestions.

Electoral assistance to the Party, therefore, became the most important task for the women's movement. The fact that the educational work of the women's movement became concentrated on such themes, however, meant the disappearance of the socialist alternative to the capitalist order. As voters, the proletarians were not given a fundamental choice for or against the capitalist system, but could only decide between the more far-reaching socio-political demands of Social Democracy and the conservative programme. With this shift in the emphasis of social democratic agitation among women from radical attempts at emancipation which went beyond

election campaign in bourgeois society, the women's movement trod
the path which led to its integration into this society, but which
cheated it of emancipation.

At the Jena Party Conference of 1905 women were given the
right to pay voluntary contributions to their *Vertrauensperson*,
and these were receipted with special stamps. Questionnaires were
distributed with the aim of registering politically organized women.
From August 1905 to July 1906, 4,933 women made voluntary
contributions, compared with barely 1,000 the year before. The
readership of *Die Gleichheit* also doubled in this period. The
'unpolitical' educational associations had 8,890 members, compared
to 3,000 before 1905.[60] At the Party Conference following the
women's conference, Clara Zetkin made a detailed speech on the
socialist attitude to the family, in which she put forward the theories
with which we have already dealt.

The year 1907 saw a Social Democratic Conference in Essen,
as well as an International Socialist Congress and the first International Socialist Women's Conference in Stuttgart. The Socialist
Congress once again adopted a resolution on female suffrage. In
justifying it Clara Zetkin said that such a right did not derive from
ideological or ethical considerations, nor should it be regarded as
the solution to all social impediments, since it left private property
intact, but that it was a 'consequence of our understanding of the
class struggle'. The proletariat would never win its political and
economic battles without the help of the women.[61] Whereas the
Party used formal democratic arguments to justify women's suffrage,
Clara Zetkin retained the perspective of the class struggle.

The next women's conference met in Nürnberg in 1908. The
discussion centred on the new position of women in the organization of the Party and the abolition of the Prussian Combination
Act. The new Combination Act for the Reich permitted women to
join political parties. Accordingly, the organizational section of
the Party constitution specified in §4 that organizations with women
members must grant the latter representation on the executive
and that female executive members should engage, with the agreement of the entire association, primarily in agitation among women.
'The Social Democratic women have thus been incorporated into
the organization of the Party throughout the Reich.'[62] The women
discussed the problems involved in cooperating with men on the
executives, and resolved to take advantage of all the opportunities

C

offered by the new constitution. Apart from this, a lot of time was spent on questions of socialist education, on which Käthe Dunker and Clara Zetkin spoke.[63] In 1911, the first international women's conference to propagate women's suffrage was held. On the same day, Social Democratic women demonstrated in all the provinces for universal suffrage. The 'Central *Vertrauensperson*' of the German women comrades had two-and-a-half million leaflets printed to publicize women's suffrage. *Die Gleichheit*, now printing more than a hundred thousand copies, likewise published an appeal.[64]

The continuous success, not only of the women's organization, but of the entire working class movement in the previous twenty-five years seemed to open up favourable perspectives for the future. Approximately 190,000 women were members of trade unions, 140,000 were members of the Social Democratic Party, the circulation of *Die Gleichheit* had reached 112,000 and there had been considerable improvements in the protection of women workers. Progress in these fields, however, was offset by serious negative developments within the Party. The great theoretical decisiveness and rhetorical sting employed by Rosa Luxemburg and Clara Zetkin in combating the revisionist tendency in the party frequently induced the Party leaders who were attacked to discriminate against women by means of malicious witticism. Thus they would respond to such criticism by pointing to the weakness of the women's movement and its simultaneous demand for equal rights. They accused the women, on the one hand, of the fact that their theory and agitational practice was not bringing corresponding successes in the form of numerical growth for the women's movement, while stating, on the other, that things could not be too bad as regards the oppression of the female sex if it could find spokesmen of such quality.[65]

Symptomatic of this inherently contradictory defensive ploy on the part of the men were the comments of Ignaz Auer at the Mainz Party Conference of 1900: 'Of course the nervous excitement of our women is, regrettably, easy enough to understand if we remember that despite years of exhausting work they have only had minimal success.'

The trouble is that there are too few women comrades in the Party. I wish there were many more. The few who have to do all the work are overloaded and thus prone to become bad-tempered. So it comes about that they sometimes make life miserable for us, even though we are not to blame.[66]

By the use of deliberate wit, which, as the minutes record, always evoked the sought-for 'merriment' of the audience, the women were put in their place with the remark that they ought first to prove themselves for a change and not vent their ill-humour concerning the lack of success of the women's movement on their innocent comrades in the Party. The discrimination which was deliberately practised against women in the Party, and of which Mrs Kähler gave examples at the Gotha Party Conference in 1896,[67] was in this way glossed over, while the existing antagonisms concerning the theory and tactics of the Party as a whole were obscured by accusing the women of griping and not achieving anything. Such an accusation was levelled against Clara Zetkin at the Stuttgart Party Conference in 1898, after she had criticized the central organ of the Party, *Vorwärts*.

Even at this early stage, Auer replied to Clara Zetkin's strong attack on the Party executive in the same tone when, amidst laughter from the audience, he said: 'If that is the oppressed sex, then what on earth will happen when they are free and enjoy equal rights.'[68] The merriment which the Party executive aroused through its counter-criticism served diversionary ends, by which dissatisfaction at the ruling state of affairs in the Party was ridiculed. The critics were accused of using revolutionary phrases which were not backed by organizational strength. When Clara Zetkin, alluding to the antagonism between the right-wing and the left said:

'They say that they want to combat revolutionary phraseology, but what they do in fact, is make the widest possible use of opportunistic phrases',[69] this was equally applicable to the attitude towards criticism of the Party from the women's movement. The fact that this criticism was made to look ridiculous also meant a break with revolutionary theory; the break with this theory, on the other hand, in turn affected the leading representatives of the women's movement. The women were already familiar with this method, as is shown by one of Mrs Kähler's comments at the Gotha Party Conference: 'Many comrades make such a joke of the woman question that we really have to ask ourselves: Are those really Party comrades who advocate equal rights?'[70] Such joking proved an effective means of discriminating against women's demands. It was an expansion of the patriarchism of the men and blunted the women's criticism of the Party's reformist practice, thus testifying to the difference between the Party's official theory and the real attitude of the Party bureaucracy to equal rights for women.

There are thus indications of a reactionary turn in developments after the abolition of the Anti-Socialist Law, despite the radical theory of women's emancipation, improvements in the protection of women workers and the successes of the Social Democratic women's movement. They became evident in the attempt to neutralize the women's movement politically, in the conflict surrounding the *Vertrauenspersonen*, in the shifting grounds given for demanding women's suffrage, and in the mocking patriarchal treatment of women at the Party Conferences. There is reason to ask, therefore, what changes had taken place in the Party which allowed this reaction not only to arise, but to become prominent.

The Anti-Socialist Law had forced the Social Democrats into the strictest observance of legality. Their powers had not been adequate to defy the prohibition of the Party organization. The declaration of struggle 'with all available means' at the Party Conference in Schloss Wyden[71] in 1880 did nothing to change the practice of respecting the law, and in view of the real relations of power it was purely rhetorical. In the period of persecution, the Party's leadership was transferred to the Reichstag caucus, the only Party body in Germany able to function. By this process, the parliamentary character of Social Democracy became stronger. With the state of emergency, the trade unions became increasingly significant for the party, for they could at least keep up the fight on the economic front.

> The growth of the wage-movement at the end of the eighties and the fact that the local trade unions were the only legal forms of organization at all, led to the convergence of all the forces of the working-class movement on the trade unions.[72]

The abolition of the Anti-Socialist Law in 1890 coincided with the establishment of the General Commission of Trade Unions, which must be seen as the working class's response to the concentration and intermeshing of industry following national unification. However, the heavy increase in votes for Social Democracy on the one hand, and the economic slump of the early nineties on the other, preserved the traditional pre-eminence of the Party over the trade unions.[73]

While the Party executive regarded the General Commission as superfluous because of its relative impotence, the 'youth opposition' in the Party held the view that the trade unions were the focal point of the organization of the proletariat and could help to prevent 'the party getting bogged down in Parliamentarism'.[74]

The revival of strike activity in 1896 showed that the Social Democratic organization could, with its press and collection lists for strike assistance, admittedly balance out many of the shortcomings of the trade-union apparatus of the time; on the other hand, however, it showed that Social Democracy, with its 2 million voters and its parliamentary caucus could 'not by any means compensate for the weakness of the workers when faced by the employers in the factories.'[75] These experiences forced the trade unions to centralize and introduce strict discipline. Whereas from 1891 to 1901 trade union membership only rose from 278,000 to 678,000, it shot up to 2,340,000 from 1901 to 1911.[76]

> In 1913, the trade unions had ten times as many members as in 1895, and the increase in paid trade-union officials was greater than the increase in the number of members. In one decade, the number of trade-union employees grew more than five times as fast as the number of members.[77]

The growth of the trade unions reinforced the efforts of the trade-union leadership to get rid of the bonds that tied them to Social Democracy. Whereas the neutrality of the trade unions had previously made sense in tactical, legal terms, the General Council was now able to proclaim their actual neutrality on principle. The conflict over sovereignty in the working-class movement was resolved in favour of the trade unions through the outcome of the debate on the political mass strike. The Party was forced to retract the support it had already given to this notion, and the General Council was even able to prohibit discussion on the subject.[78] In 1906, 'the Mannheim Party Conference for the first time formally granted the trade unions the right of decision in all critical situations'.[79]

The hegemony of the trade unions in the working-class movement led ultimately to the policy by which the war was not rejected on 4 August 1914 for the further reason that a refusal to comply would have led to the dissolution of their organization and the confiscation of their assets. After a decade in which 'the rise of the trade-union organization had been exemplary . . . the argument was still adhered to that: what we need most of all for the extension of our organization is peace'.[80]

The development of the working-class movement between 1890 and 1914 was marked by the heavy growth and increasing predominance of the trade unions in crucial matters. Despite the increase in its members and voters, Social Democracy remained impotent in parliament. The trade unions, in contrast, had considerable success in improving working conditions, in reducing working hours and in their fight for better wages. Their growing apparatus formed the livelihood for numerous officials, editors and employees. Their establishments (houses, publishing firms, printing works) amounted to considerable assets. They lost members only in times of crisis, while it was precisely in such periods that Social Democracy increased its strength. While the Party was still debating the role of the trade unions in the class struggle, the latter were already starting to cooperate with the authorities of the bourgeois state.[81] The bureaucratization of the working-class movement steadily grew.[82] The conflict between 'revisionism' and 'orthodoxy' had the ground taken from under its feet even more by the practical reformist policy of the decisive section of the working-class movement, the trade unions.

Even if, as Sering suggests, the strata which agreed with the internal distribution of power in pre-war Germany only constituted a minority of the people and the inner tensions were too strong to enable the formation of a 'unified national consciousness', the strength of the state apparatus, the prestige gained by its successes abroad, the upswing in the economy and the 'considerable semi-democratic safety-valves of the constitutional regime' were enough to prevent the formation of any genuinely revolutionary forces . . . Although it is true that, even after the fall of the Anti-Socialist Law, the working-class movement remained 'outside the official nation', it had never, despite its revolutionary claims, 'consciously prepared for the struggle for power', but instead restricted itself to the 'representation of interests' and relied on 'developments'.[83]

The indications of a reactionary development that we observed in the divergence between the radical theory of women's emancipation and the practice of the Party must be viewed in the light of this general process of change in the working-class movement. The preponderance of the trade unions' economic struggle put the organization of the working class on to the path of gradual improvements in the living conditions of the proletariat, enabling bureau-cratic apparatuses to come into being which condemned revolutionary theory as idealism and overrode the theoretical disputes among the Party intellectuals in order to get on with the business of the day. In a period when the intensity and productivity of labour were increasing and working hours were simultaneously being reduced, such business centred on labour legislation, social security and the wage struggle. 'The achievement of socialism was removed to the distant realm of speeches at Party Conferences and leading articles.'[84] If on the one hand, revisionism constituted a reaction to objective changes occurring within the capitalist system, on the other, as Robert Michels stresses, it had a 'causal relationship with the precociously blasé nature of disintegrative tendencies in bourgeois literature'. As Michels puts it, revisionism was the 'theoretical expression of the scepticism of the disappointed, the weary, and those who no longer believed; it was the socialism of non-socialists with a socialist past'.[85]

The corollary of this rejection of Marxism was a sceptical attitude to the emancipation of women and a stodgily benevolent but nonetheless effective rejection of women's endeavours towards cooperation on an equal basis within the Party. Because of their special situation as the disadvantaged 'Fifth Estate' at work, in society and in the Party, the politically active women in Social Democracy were frequently adherents of the revisionist theory, and consequently found themselves in the difficult position of being attacked by two overlapping fronts, that of revisionism and that of proletarian anti-feminism.[86]

Section B

5/World War, Party Split and Revolution

For years, International Social Democracy had been aware of the danger of war, and at conferences before the war this led to solemn declarations of international solidarity. Just before the war broke out, hasty efforts were made in the hope that the unity of the working class would stand the test. Internationalism lost the day, however. It was the trade unions which determined the attitude of the working-class movement. An executive conference of the free trade unions decided, at the beginning of 1914, 'immediately to break off all wages moves and to pay no strike benefits for the duration of the war'.[1] By doing this, they also decided how the Party would interpret the coming war. It would not be regarded as an imperialist war, against which the forces of the international proletariat would have to be mobilized, but as a defensive one, in which the uppermost duty of the working-class movement was to defend the fatherland. This position determined the attitude of the Social Democratic caucus to the war credits.[2] It went down in history as the 'policy of the 4th August.'

Party discipline, however, could not bridge for long the fundamental differences within the caucus. A group of radical oppositionists soon formed around Rosa Luxemburg and Karl Liebknecht, the son of Wilhelm Liebknecht, and this became 'the nucleus of the future Spartacusbund—among others, Franz Mehring, later the author of a biography of Marx and a party history, and Clara Zetkin, an organizer of women'.[3]

With Luxemburg and Zetkin, the most important Social Democratic women had departed from the official line of the Party. Of the better-known women, Käthe Dunker and Luise Zietz likewise attached themselves to the new groups. According to Hilde Lion,[4] the majority of *Gleichheit* readers sided with the radical minority in 1916. Zetkin's disenchantment with the majority Party was the outcome of her theoretical and practical work up to that time. Her standing and influence no doubt contributed to the fact that many women were drawn into the camp opposing war. It is also likely that the discrepancy between the Party's feminist theory and its discrimination against women in political practice was food for the opposition. Men's resistance to female labour, which we have described as proletarian anti-feminism, and the divergence between the Social Democratic theory of women's emancipation and Party practice have a common root: the two-fold character of women's emancipation under capitalism. On the one hand, women were freed from male tutelage in the family by being drawn into the process of production. On the other, this emancipation put pressure on wages and increased the distress of the working-class family. This resulted in proletarian anti-feminism, which sought to abolish female labour and which was only slowly discarded by the working-class movement. However, female labour also brought new members to political and trade union organizations and thus strengthened the hand of the proletariat. The socialist theory of emancipation had relied on this effect of female labour more than anything. The same willingness and docility which made women sought after by the employers, however, also meant that women were not very interested in trade-union or political organization.

Not even the Party theory could overcome the traditional male prejudice against women's attempts to emancipate themselves. For when women's emancipation took the form of female labour, it increased competition among workers. In periods of prosperity, the women's movement fought for higher wages and better-paid positions, but in times of crisis it had to fight for work as such. Although in the factories the workers possessed few means to prevent female labour, they were in a better position to resist women's advance towards responsible positions within the Party.

The mechanism of competition, of which the men were helpless victims in the economic sphere, was carried over into the working-class movement, one of whose aims was, however, the abolition of competition. There were too few women members, and the theory of equal rights seemed to demand the surrender of male privileges far too directly, for the Party to be able to hold its own against the special status of men, their fear of being pushed out and of losing prestige.

The two-fold nature of women's emancipation under capitalism thus consisted in the fact that while women could emancipate themselves by going out to work, competition at the same time imposed limits on this emancipation. Women, it is true, proved time and again that they were qualified to do jobs of which they had previously been thought incapable. But the men clung to the view that such cases were exceptions, and the genuine backwardness of the female sex continued to be used to justify discrimination against women. The socialist theory of women's liberation failed to make the workers aware of the fact that they were playing into the employers' hands by carrying over into the working-class movement the same antagonism that capital had aroused between male and female labour.

It was not until 1931, at the Leipzig Party Conference of the SPD, that the rejection of female labour was recognized for what it was: 'an attempt to create a conflict of workers amongst each other'.[5]

Toni Pfülf, a Social Democratic MP in the Weimar period, had tried, in contrast, to explain it purely in psychological terms. She wrote:

> Intellectually, the Social Democrats advocate individual development, and economic and social liberation for women, for they know the danger that its opposite poses for socialist development. But in its heart of hearts, the great majority of the organized work force does not favour liberation. . . . Sexual pride wins out over principles.[6]

Toni Pfülf completely overlooks the economic roots of the resistance to equal rights for women. The fact that men feared competition from women more than from their own kind was not the result of 'sexual pride' stemming from a patriarchal society, but was due above all to the lower wages paid to women, which made them sought-after employees.

To that extent, therefore, the precondition for a positive attitude towards female labour and towards women's co-operation in the Party on an equal basis lay in an adequate understanding of the way in which the capitalist economy operates. Where this did not exist, the working-class movement fell prey to proletarian anti-feminism, and even within the Party conformed to the general discrimination against women.

Rosa Luxemburg's treatment in the Party offers a further interesting example of this. Marie Juchacz describes how Rosa

Luxemburg was made to feel men's fear of competition. In a letter
to Bebel, Luxemburg wrote that from the outset she had had a
strange reception in German Social Democracy. Her appointment
to the position of editor of the Leipzig paper, *Die Arbeiterzeitung*,
in 1898, sparked off a rebellion against her, and she encountered
similar difficulties in the course of her editorial work for the
Leipziger Volkszeitung. 'People were loth to grant a "woman" the
same powers as her male predecessors.'[7]

On the one hand, therefore, women were probably pressed
into opposition because they were clearly discriminated against
even within the working-class movement itself. On the other
hand, decades of consistent agitation by Clara Zetkin in *Die
Gleichheit*, at women's conferences and in the Party meant that
the partly latent, partly acute dissatisfaction felt by many women
had already been formulated theoretically and activated politically.
The war policy then brought them into open conflict with the
majority Party. Their entry into the production process on a
massive scale also helped to radicalize the trade unions, a fact
that cannot be explained, as Preller thinks, solely by the notion
that these new workers 'lacked long years of experience'.

> The psychological burdens of the war which women in particular
> had to bear as wives, mothers and sisters of soldiers, as housewives
> facing the difficulties of food production, and as mothers of small
> children growing up without their fathers, and the physical
> demands which women, like all those who stayed at home, had
> imposed on them by the increasing shortage of food, were now
> made even worse by physical and psychological exertion at work.
> Many of the jobs they now did had not only been closed to
> them before and were therefore alien, but often demanded such
> feats of strength and involved such damage to health, that it was
> possible, and indeed inevitable, that the power of the nation,
> which resides in women, would be damaged in the most serious
> manner.[8]

Up to the outbreak of war, *Die Gleichheit* shared its anti-
militarism and fundamental rejection of imperialist war with the
other Social Democratic papers. Whereas the latter propagated the
party truce, however, *Die Gleichheit* retained its stance even after
the war had broken out. It steadily reported peace demonstrations
by Social Democratic women, who for the reasons outlined above,
offered greater resistance than men to the official Party line. Admittedly, after the start of the war, *Die Gleichheit* like other papers

published an appeal by the Party executive and the General Commission of Trade Unions for the organized women to support the 'Relief Action', asking them to distribute information on the state's claims on people remaining behind in the War, and to assist in community care for the children, the sick and women in childbirth. But even if *Die Gleichheit*, for reasons of Party discipline, could not refuse to have anything to do with this programme, it nonetheless consistently emphasized women's desire for peace.[9]

Meanwhile, any fundamental discussion was prohibited because of the agreement on a party truce reached between the Government and the Party and trade unions. On 4 September 1914 *Die Gleichheit* noted with resignation:

> The martial law which is in force makes it impossible for us to seek a conscientious answer to the question: did it have to be? It prevents us from showing up plainly the social forces whose inexorable rule has dashed the hopes and desires of the millions in all countries who have now been dragged into the tornado of the war.[10]

The prohibition of any discussion on the cause of the war in the press, however, did not prevent *Die Gleichheit* from expressing, as far as was possible, its opposition to the war. The frequency with which this brought it into conflict with the censorship is shown by the increasing amounts of blank space in its columns, which were demonstratively left standing by the editorial board. Clara Zetkin was one of the organizers of the International Women's Conference in Bern in 1915, which did not have the approval of the Party, but in which citizens of almost all the belligerent countries took part.[11] *Die Gleichheit* was internationally recognized as the organ of women opposed to the war (as early as 1907, a 'central office' for the 'International Bureau of Socialist Women of All Countries' had been set up within the editorial board[12], and lines ran from its offices to Switzerland, England, France and the United States and many other countries. Obviously, the radicalization of women did not remain unnoticed among the reformist majority of the Party. August 1915 not only saw the arrest of Clara Zetkin,[13] but also the start of counter-measures by the Party. In 1915, *Die Gleichheit* reported on the conflict of opinion of which it was itself the subject and published letters both agreeing with and rejecting its position.[14]

After the oppositional Social Democrats had joined together

to form the 'Social Democratic Working Group', which described itself as the 'old Social Democracy', their tendency was condemned by the executive and committee of the Party.[15] Shortly afterwards, Luise Zietz was expelled from the Party executive. For the moment, *Die Gleichheit* remained in the hands of the Party's opposition. There was still time to protest against the expulsion of Luise Zietz as an 'infringement of the Party's constitution', but in its 16th issue it had to publish a rebuttal of her basic attitude by the executive and committee of the Party. Clara Zetkin was forced to resign the editorship. The Party executive took over and appointed Marie Juchacz, and later Clara Bohm-Schuch, as the responsible editor. A letter was published in issue 16, which prepared for the change in editorship as follows:

> In our area *Die Gleichheit* has lost almost all its subscribers. Our women don't want it at all. Even before the war, the articles were unpalatable for the great majority of women workers. We need a popular women's magazine. Otherwise, the trade union and local papers will take from us the chance of a women's paper for the Party as a whole.[16]

The 18th issue of the 1916/1917 volume bore a new subtitle, which read 'Magazine for the interests of workers' wives and women workers'. The programme of the new editors was for 'political education, simple teaching and valuable entertainment'.[17] Symptomatic of the new spirit of the magazine was its report on the National Conference of Social Democratic Women in 1917, which stated:

> The conference was not completely drenched, as such conferences usually are, in radical verbiage. This did not mean that the cause of the class struggle and the upward and forward march of the working class was served any less by the conference. In fact it was thereby served with much greater energy.[18]

The conference discussed the problems of women in the war economy, agitation and women's suffrage. Apart from the special conditions of female labour during the war there was nothing new about this; it had all been discussed by the women's movement before. The lack of radical 'verbiage' certainly made itself felt in the fact that no clear stand was taken on the war. This, however, not only did not serve the 'cause of the workers', but it did harm. The sole aim of the report in *Die Gleichheit* was to bring Clara Zetkin into disrepute. The rejection of 'radical verbiage', which was allegedly a precondition for effective work, was meant to be a blow at the renegade Zetkin. The substance of this attack becomes clear if we compare the alleged 'upward and forward march of the working-class movement' with the fact that the latter had, on the contrary, been weakened by the split in its ranks and that the strength of the movement really found expression in the resistance to the official policy. Instead of uniting in a common denunciation of the war, the Party deepened the rift by its campaign against Zetkin. The common ground which still existed, despite everything, was obscured by the disintegration of the organization and by personal animosity. In 1917, Majority Social Democracy and the Independent German Social Democratic Party (USPD)* basically wanted one and the same thing: 'A constitutional opposition to the Imperial Government with the object of achieving peace.'[19]

At this time Clara Zetkin, like Bernstein, belonged to the USPD. The conflict between the various socialist tendencies did not break out again until the war had ended, when it led to the dissolution of the USPD. The opposing groups polarized into the SPD and the KPD. Characteristically, the common peace policy of the Majority Party and the Independents which alone made the coalition of 10 November 1918 possible did nothing to stop the campaign of hate pursued by Social Democracy against Clara Zetkin. Even though she was not a member of the Spartacus League and only went over to the Communists after Social Democracy had betrayed the Revolution, she was accused time and again of being incapable or too radical. She was never forgiven the fact that she had drawn the consequences from the policy·in which she had believed in 1914, and which at that time was at least tolerated by the Party, even if not without contradiction, while the official women's movement had remained passive.

In July 1919, *Die Gleichheit* settled accounts with its past and

* The Independent Social Democratic Party (USPD) began as an opposition group within the Social Democratic Reichstag caucus and voted against the war credits in December 1915. They were subsequently expelled from the Party and with their supporters formed a new Party (the USPD) in 1917. The old Party came to be referred to as the Majority Socialists. The issue that caused the Party split—the war credits—cut across many more significant differences within the Party, and many diverse figures such as Bernstein, Kautsky and Zetkin found themselves together in the ranks of the USPD. Little, apart from this one issue, separated the two Parties, but they failed to re-unite until 1922. By then, the real differences within the pre-war SPD had assumed tangible form in the opposition between the KPD (the Communist Party) and the Social Democrats.—*Translator*

published a defence of its new course. Of the Zetkin era, it wrote:

> Generally speaking, the magazine was also eagerly read, but it
> became increasingly evident as time passed that the majority of
> women, especially the new ones streaming in, did not understand
> it, since the style of *Die Gleichheit* presupposed great intellectual
> experience on the part of the reader. Comrade Zetkin, who is owed
> a great deal by the women's movement, wrote the magazine in
> a manner that did not do justice to the needs of the masses who
> had no intellectual or political background. Only a relatively small
> number of women comrades could entirely follow Comrade
> Zetkin's style and thought processes. Ultimately, however, a large
> number also came to disapprove of her political views. The result
> was a decline in women's interest in *Die Gleichheit*, and a simul-
> taneous drop in the circulation of the magazine.[20]

The contradiction between the policies of Clara Zetkin and
the Party executive was not brought out into the open, nor was it
made clear that the conflict which had erupted concerned quite
fundamental differences between the left and right wings, originat-
ing in the revisionism controversy and sparked off by the 'policy of
the 4th August'. Instead, Clara Zetkin was accused of failing to
edit *Die Gleichheit* in line with the 'needs of the masses who had
no intellectual or political background', even though her aim had
been precisely to educate such people. Instead of pointing out the
particular revolutionary character of her policy, the article accused
her of the ineffectiveness of this policy. She was made responsible
for the fall in circulation, while the decline of the entire working-
class movement as a result of the war was deliberately glossed
over.[21] Besides, the circulation of *Die Gleichheit* had deliberately
been reduced by the counter-propaganda of the Party and the trade
unions. Even under the new editorship, however, *Die Gleichheit*
never recovered its former circulation. On the contrary, in 1920 it
declined to 20,000 less than in 1917, when the low figure was
allegedly the fault of Clara Zetkin.[22]

In 1916 the majority of *Die Gleichheit*'s readership still sided
with the radical minority, but later more and more subscribers
changed to the *Gewerkschaftliche Frauenzeitung* (*Women's Trade
Union Paper*), which reached a distribution of 100,000 only a year
after its inception. It first appeared at the start of 1916, published
by Carl Legien, the trade-union leader, and edited by Gertrude
Hanna. The paper was designed to win women for the trade-union
movement now that political education was no longer a priority

and discussion of trade-union problems had acquired a totally new significance through the development of female labour over the previous 25 years.[23] The predominant influence of the trade unions in the working-class movement, which we described at the end of the first section, is once more underlined by the programme of this paper. The accent on 'trade union problems' and the neglect of 'political education' did not simply accord with the nature of the *Frauenzeitung* as a trade-union paper; it represented at the same time a weapon in the fight against the revolutionary anti-war policy of Clara Zetkin. The fact that the *Frauenzeitung* came to be seen as a competing venture to *Die Gleichheit* is proved, for example, by the fact that in Württemburg the Social Democratic women recommended it instead of *Die Gleichheit*.[24] It sided with the majority in the Party. As a result, it was not haunted by the censors in the way *Die Gleichheit* was. In contrast to the decline of *Die Gleichheit* and the female membership of the Party, the *Gewerkschaftliche Frauenzeitung* managed to increase its circulation to 100,000 by 1917.[25]

The Party split weakened the Social Democratic women's movement considerably. After a membership drive by the Party executive in October 1917 there was, it is true, an increase in the number of women members,[26] but at the Women's Conference in 1919 Marie Juchacz was forced to admit that 'the party split had deprived us of many of our forces'.[27] Mrs Kähler explained why this was so: 'They (the women) have increasingly moved to the left-wing of the Party, and therefore, even today, the attitude of the USPD seems much more acceptable to them than what we tell them.'[28]

This weakness, however, was not considered as crucial to the progress of the women's movement as the increase in female labour resulting from the war. In this situation, which constituted a setback for the Party, comfort was sought in the fact that the women's cause had taken an 'objective' step forward, but at the same time there was a mistaken belief that the successes would prove durable. A notice in the *Gewerkschaftliche Frauenzeitung* shows that the war economy was unable to provide work for all the women who were looking for jobs:

According to a report in the State Employment Gazette, on 1 March (1917) 3,973,457 women and 3,962,625 men were enrolled in the health insurance schemes registered with the Department.

This means that 10,382 more women than men have jobs. Despite this fact, there is still a glut of female labour. According to a report from the Department of Employment, in February of this year there were 112 female and 62 male applicants for a single job.[29]

Even when the war was in its third year, the military call-up for men and the 'Auxiliary Service Act' were still insufficient to satisfy the female demand for jobs. Despite this, the war substantially increased both the absolute number of working women and their number as a percentage of the total work force. The number of working women had risen from 9.5 million before the war to approximately 15 million.[30] Women had penetrated into occupations and were doing work that had previously been closed to them, and they had proved that they were no less efficient than men in these spheres.

> Male employment declined as a result of the army's heavy demands. . . .[31] In 1913, women made up about 20 per cent of the total work force; until 1918, women's wages rose more than men's, and in that year they again rose more. Some of these wage-increases were due to the fact that women were now employed in industries where the wages were normally higher than in the previously 'customary women's industries', such as textiles and clothing.[32]

The fierce debate in the Party during the war surrounding the concept of 'war socialism' proves that there was no widespread awareness of the fact that the apparent approximation of economic measures and social developments to socialist goals was merely the outcome of the controlled economy of the war.

> Only the full deployment of state power and carefully planned organization was capable of preventing prices rising and food-stuffs finding their way into the rich suburbs while starving masses revolted in front of empty shops in the working-class areas. Thus the first attempt was made during the war to regulate the economy from above in accordance with needs. The results were pitiful. From the standpoint of propaganda, therefore, it was a monstrous error on the part of the Social Democrats to give it the label of 'war socialism'. Meat, sugar, fat and soap disappeared while the starry-eyed theorists triumphantly declared that this state of affairs was a kind of socialism.[33]

Because women were taking a much greater part than before the war in production and community and state welfare programmes, they were easily tempted to translate the war-time emergency measures into a step forward for the women's movement. The grounds given for women's suffrage at the Würzburg Party Conference must be seen in the same context, for it was explained that since women were everywhere being drawn into co-operation with men, they should also be given the right of co-determination.[34]

The extent to which the Social Democrats identified themselves with the Imperial Government can be seen from the words of Wally Zepler, a leading woman Social Democrat, who wrote in 1919:

> Quite rightly the military successes of our country are not least attributed to the intellectual capability of the individual within the mass army, and to the educational force of the working-class organization as one of the sources of this ability.[35]

The Social Democrats were so involved in their joint responsibility in the leadership of the war that their criticism of the ruling system was muffled and turned instead into pride about Social Democracy's success in 'educating the German soldier'. Indeed, the system was even said to have socialist traits.

Social Democracy's attitude to the 1918 Revolution was determined by the structural and functional changes that the Party had undergone before the war. The party split, which was not shown for what it really was until the breakaway of the left wing after 1918, had its roots not only in the policy of 4 August, but also in other events that had taken place earlier: bureaucratization, the predominance of the trade unions in the working-class movement, the revision of socialist theory, the dichotomy between the Party's theory and its reformist practice, and a lack of clarity about the Party's tasks after the war, especially in the economic sphere. When the Social Democrats refused to put themselves at the head of the revolutionary workers, and instead opposed their demands with a policy of maintaining order, the Revolution came to an end with the overthrow of the monarchy. A Council of People's Deputies was formed in November 1918 and entrusted with the powers of government, but even though it was made up entirely of Socialists and finally gave women the vote, the elections to the National Assembly, which took place on 19 January 1919, failed to give the two Socialist parties a majority. They won only 185 of the 421 seats, and 22 of these went to the Independents.[36] The Socialists failed to exploit the period of the Interregnum to lay the foundations for the order they desired, and the women voters failed to make the hoped-for use of their new right. 36 women, of whom 18 were Social Democrats, took their seats in the National Assembly. But their predominant emotions were those of impotence, disappointment and resignation. It was, admittedly, said at the Weimar Party Conference in 1919, that the extension of the suffrage to women had fundamentally changed women's status.[37] Marie Juchacz, on the other hand, stated:

> The revolution has introduced women to parliamentarism. This has deprived our movement of valuable forces. . . . I must say, however, that I had a completely different idea about what it would be like in parliament. I had imagined that it would be productive, and that an abundance of ideas would pour down upon us like a rich summer shower. Unfortunately, I must say that my own experience tells me that this is not so. Previously, we would read the paper and adopt an attitude to what happened and wonder why things in parliament were done in such and such a way and not otherwise. Now the women who have remained outside ought to come to our aid with suggestions. Certainly, a great deal of work will be done for the waste paper basket. But even the petitions and proposals that suffer this fate are not always without their uses. All such thoughts live on, and in some form or other they one day assume a tangible form . . . The economic dependence of women still exists as previously.[38]

And later, in her biography of important Social Democratic women, she wrote:

> We were somewhat unprepared when finally confronted with the fact of women's suffrage. In the preceding years we had been forced to restrict ourselves to the exposure of social harms and demands that they be remedied. The war, it is true, gave many of us the chance to take a strong hand in social and community work. But it was precisely this which made us recognize that the bourgeois women's movement was much better equipped to 'do such work, for their average educational background was higher than ours and their material means were more abundant. For us socialists, this recognition was shattering.[39]

It could not fail to be recognized that although women's entry into parliament fulfilled a time-old Social Democratic demand, the women remained just as far from their emancipation thereafter as society as a whole. The possibilities of parliamentary work were inevitably disappointing. The distribution of political power made it impossible for them to achieve their goals immediately, while the half-hearted revolution and the need to eradicate the results of the war perpetually hampered a start even on the most rudimentary socio-political legislation. The Socialist women's forty years experience in organizing the female proletariat crumbled before the demands of parliamentary practice. Apart from this, Social Democracy had lost many of its most gifted women through death and the Party split.[40]

The achievement of women's suffrage signalled the end of the heroic epoch of the Socialist women's movement. The women who led the Social Democratic women's movement from 1919 to 1939 differed fundamentally from the older generation of fighters for the cause of socialist revolution and women's liberation. They failed to distinguish themselves through outstanding achievements in the theoretical field (Luxemburg), the sharpness of their words, basic organizational work or impassioned educational campaigns to spread the revolutionary idea (Zetkin, Zietz, Baader). In line with the new constitution of the Party as a state-supportive mass organization with a reformist orientation, their work lay in the 'details' of the schools service, the trade unions, workers' welfare, councils and parliament. The politics of day-to-day tactical moves in parliament inclined them 'to regard socialism more as a subject for proletarian ceremonies than as a burning problem of economic policy here and now'.[41]

The achievement of the revolutionary programme of German Social Democracy, as formulated by Kautsky as late as 1891 in Erfurt, was hampered by the success of the working-class movement in obtaining legislation, the change in the methods of capitalism and the rise of a working-class bureaucracy which was prepared to cooperate with bourgeois institutions.

The women's movement shared in the successes of the working-class movement as a whole since it was a part of it, but it could also record its own particular steps forward.

As far back as the preceding century women had been assured of their right to work through Social Democracy's rejection of anti-feminism and the beginnings of protection for women workers. In 1908, they had been granted admission to the political parties. After the war, they were given the suffrage and men and women were declared to have equal rights 'both in public and in the family'. The Constitution required 'the removal of all exceptional regulations against women public servants'.[42] Admittedly, equal rights in private law were only proclaimed after 1945, with corresponding clauses written into the Constitutions of both parts of Germany.[43]

The persistence of women's social inequality in the Weimar Republic, however, revealed the incongruity between formal equal rights and actual emancipation.

Equal status under law proved to be a means of preserving social inequality. The fight against the economic system, which was the root cause of inequality, was made ineffective by the appearance that women now had equal access to all opportunities and that they only needed to take the initiative to stride through the opened barriers.

6/The Decline of the Women's Movement until the end of the Inflationary Period

a/Women in the Post-War Economy

After the outbreak of the war, many branches of peace-time industry were laid idle, and because the men were called up for service in an irregular fashion, this led initially to heavy unemployment. The women were particularly badly affected. Whereas male unemployment had already returned to its peace-time proportions as early as May 1915, unemployment among women was not reduced until the introduction of the Auxiliary Service Act at the close of 1916. In enterprises with more than nine workers engaged in mining, manual labour, building and industry there were only 71.6 per cent as many male employees in 1918 as there were in 1913, while female employment, in contrast, had risen to 152 per cent of the 1913 level. These 'advances' in female labour were offset by drastic reductions in the protection of women workers.

> Special protection for women, young people and children, as well as the hygienic maximum working day, were dropped from the industrial code, limits were placed on the services of sick-funds, and mandatory insurance for outworkers was abolished. Freedom of association remained in the civil code, but regulations requiring military approval imposed serious limitations upon it.[1]

Despite the fact that the number of women workers increased both absolutely and relatively during the war years, therefore, their situation did not improve at all. Rather, their rights as workers were curtailed. The increase in female labour would only have been an advance towards emancipation if it had become a durable state of affairs and had brought with it all the consequences for industrial law and wage agreements. However, it was far too obviously connected with the war economy for there to be any likelihood of this. The post-war economy rapidly led to the 'normalization' of women's share in the labour force.

> In considering German economic life during the revolutionary period two main manifestations of the crisis must be distinguished —the permanent crisis in German political economy that developed as a result of the World War and which has persisted to the present day; the particular crisis extant at the time of the Revolution and the end of the war. The permanent crisis in German economic life is due to the fact that a densely populated industrial country with comparatively limited territory, like Germany, is dependent upon foreign countries for its means of livelihood . . . Quite apart from the reparation demands of the Entente, it was a hopeless task for German industry after 1918 to find any means of paying for the foreign supplies that were a vital necessity to the German people . . . German industry had, until November, 1918, been engaged in making war material. The demand for this suddenly ceased, and it was necessary to readjust industry to peace-time conditions. Relations between German manufacturers and their foreign customers had, needless to say, been broken off, and were not easy to re-establish. There was every probability of serious unemployment.[2]

The expected standstill in the armaments industry after the end of the war and the preparations for regulating female labour during the period of the so-called transitional economy provoked several discussions in 1918 on topics such as the suggestions put forward by the 'Society for Social Reform' and the 'League of German Women's Associations'.[3] As the end of the war drew nearer, trends towards unemployment and wage reductions became increasingly noticeable in the war industry. This led to discussions between workers and employers on demobilization.[4] In 1918, a Demobilization Department was set up, and a 'Central Working Group' consisting of all the leading associations was formed to regulate all questions concerning the 'transitional economy'. One principle with far-reaching consequences for women workers was that all returned servicemen were given the right of immediate reinstatement in their former jobs.[5] The Council of People's Deputies, which ruled from November 1918 until the convocation of the National Assembly in February 1919, passed measures which included a series of demobilization decrees intended to regulate the dissolution of the army and the integration of servicemen into the economy. One such decree obliged employers to dismiss anybody who was not unconditionally dependent on their wages. Women were particularly affected by the decrees of 28 March 1919 and 25 January 1920. People were to be dismissed in the following order of priority:

1   Women, whose husbands had a job.
2   Single women and girls.
3   Women and girls who had only 1–2 people to look after.
4   All other women and girls.

In 1921 the applicability of these measures was limited to areas with a minimum of 100,000 inhabitants and where the number of people on the dole was in excess of 1.5 per cent. The measures were to expire on 31 March 1922, but were extended to 31 October of the following year.[6]

In his address on 'The immediate tasks of economic policy' at the Social Democratic Party Conference in 1917, Heinrich Cunow had already pointed to the dangers of a glut on the labour market, pressure on wages and unemployment, following a sudden general demobilization. He demanded that an order of dismissals be established which would take employment opportunities into account.[7] At the Weimar Party Conference (1919), Gertrud Hanna had the following to say on the transitional economy:

> During the war, the basic direction of development in female labour has been towards sanitary protection for women and children, and different types of occupational training for women as compared to men, as well as a change in the nature of their employment. The main question now is: How can we assure women of the jobs to which they are entitled? . . . I have already pointed out before that the end of the war would inevitably bring stagnation on the labour market, irrespective of whether we won or not . . . I had no doubt whatsoever that this stagnation would inevitably make itself felt primarily among women . . . The present attitude towards female labour and the hostility towards it does not therefore correspond to a change of opinion, but is a result of the bleak conditions of the present time . . . When looking at the dismissal of women overall, we are confronted with the question: What is the lesser evil, female or male unemployment? It is quite extraordinarily difficult to answer this question.

In practice, however, it was very quickly answered, over the heads of the women and to their disadvantage. For the leading women in Social Democracy there was nothing for it but to declare their impotence, and admit, like Gertrud Hanna at the end of her address:

> As the reporter on this question, I am in the uncomfortable position of being unable to offer any suggestions as to how the woman question can be solved at the present time . . . I have only one suggestion: women must work to gain more influence over who is employed and who is dismissed.[8]

She was at a loss to say how women could increase their influence in this sphere. Although the percentage of women in the free trade unions reached its highest level for the period 1918–1931 in 1920 with 27.7 per cent, and although workers had acquired a certain share in decision-making through the establishment of factory councils, the women were powerless against the programme of dismissals ordered by the Government. Admittedly, the demobilization decrees were not aimed exclusively at women, but in practice they resulted initially in the mass dismissal of married women workers.

> Indeed, so rapid was the decline, that by March 1919 the percentage of women in the total work force was down approximately to what it had been in March 1914. Within two months, therefore, 'peace-time conditions' had been re-established.[9]

The hostility towards female labour, prevalent among the workers as a result of the high level of unemployment, did not end with the onset of the demobilization decrees. It is true that as early as 1919 the 10th Congress of Trade Unions resolved, at the instigation of Gertrud Hanna, that: 'The Congress recognizes that women have a right to jobs in line with their special nature and abilities. The trade unions have a duty to watch that hostility to women does not play any part in appointments and dismissals.'[10] Faced with the economic distress of the time, however, appeals of this kind proved just as ineffective as the subsequent official expiry of the demobilization decrees. The factory councils themselves became instruments for organized hostility to women, and through influence or force frequently had women dismissed, even against the wishes of the employers. The latter, of course, valued women who had learned their jobs during the war even more because they were also cheap labour. Such demands by workers for women to be dismissed were even the subject of an interpellation in the Reichstag, in which reference was made to pressure from the Committees of Unemployed.[11] In 1919, the *Gewerkschaftliche Frauenzeitung* published suggestions on how to 'reduce unemployment in the industrial cities and to lower friction between the male unemployed, particularly ex-servicemen, and women who are working or looking for work'. The paper called on the unemployed to help move coal, make iron, speed up the transportation of goods and to go into agriculture and forestry. It made an appeal for women to put their jobs 'at disposal'.[12]

The economy had become so disorganized that resort was being made to the completely inadequate measure of asking the unemployed to help themselves, which was at the same time meant to get languishing production moving again. This attempt to combine the provision of jobs, relief work and stepped-up production was nothing less than an admission of the bankruptcy of the economic and political ideas of Social Democracy.

The backlash from war socialism was also reflected in the proceedings of the Kassel Party Conference in 1920. Helene Grünberg reported on the way in which married women workers had been dismissed in accordance with the decrees promulgated by the Demobilization Department. She could not avoid voicing serious criticism of the measures taken by leading Party comrades.

> We must count on the fact that this will cause serious damage to the economic life of the individual family. . . . We are not creating openings for the unemployed by this means, but only increasing the misery of the working class in general.[13]

The stated aim of the Demobilization Decrees was to get the returning servicemen back into the process of production; what remained unstated was the government's intention to give the millions of soldiers an 'ordered' way of life as quickly as possible to prevent them from taking revolutionary action. For the women, however, the re-instatement of the men mostly meant quite simply the loss of their own jobs. The workers themselves regarded the Demobilization Decrees as a means of forcing women back out of their jobs. Obviously, for women who had been forced to take on heavy jobs in consequence of their obligation to do auxiliary service or because their husbands had been called up, dismissal meant an improvement in their situation. The husband's homecoming enabled them to return to their domestic set-up, which they had abandoned against their own will. Since women's wages stagnated in the post-war period, while men's wages, in contrast, went up,[14] the replacement of women workers by men was also a step forward in material terms for working-class families, but this advance was soon lost again through the rapid devaluation of money. The dismissal of women, however, made it impossible for a family to earn 'double wages' (from the work of both partners) and increasingly also for single women and those independent of their family to have a job.

If we look at the Demobilization Decrees and their effect on female labour from the viewpoint of women's emancipation as striven for by socialist theory, our judgement must be negative; for women's dismissal from heavy labour, to which they were unsuited, stood in contrast to the trend for women to be squeezed out of production more and more, except in the expressly female occupations.

Quite apart from this, the dismissal of women increased the rivalry between male and female workers and reinforced proletarian anti-feminism (caused by the capitalist relations of production). Gertrud Hanna therefore offered the following judgement :

> Until relatively recently, as long as there was widespread unemployment, the demand was often made, with the backing of the law, that married women be dismissed regardless. The justification was the time-honoured one that the woman's place was in the home. No one cared, or even asked, whether the women's livelihood was looked after, and sometimes no one even cared whether or not someone was really appointed to fill the job of the woman who had been fired; often, the job remained completely vacant. It was not the intention of the originators, nor is it in the interests of the working class, and especially of the trade unions, that the regulations should be applied in this way, and not seldom so applied at the instigation of the organized workers. . . . The intention was to make available the jobs of men and women who were not unconditionally dependent on their wages, and it was primarily designed to help the unemployed ex-servicemen. . . . In a period when the campaign being waged against female labour exceeds anything known for years in the working-class movement, it is surely understandable that the attempt to interest women in trade-union tasks has not exactly met with success.[15]

The expulsion of women from jobs which they had taken up during the war, the decline in the percentage of women in the total work force to the pre-war level, and the increase in anti-feminist attitudes, dominated the women's movement in the first five years after the war. The movement's decline was reflected in the drop in female membership of the Party and in the circulation figures of the women's papers. It demonstrated the ineffectiveness of constitutional equal rights. The social policy of the People's Deputies, the universally binding nature of wage agreements, the introduction of the eight-hour day, the code for domestic workers, and the establishment of care for the unemployed, to name only the most important innovations, were similarly proved ineffective in the years following the war.

Because the workers were dependent on parliamentary democracy to achieve their social demands, the fate of social legislation hinged on whether they or the employers were successful in obtaining influence over the state. The crisis which overshadowed the first year of the Republic, however, prevented any strengthening of the working-class movement, and as early as June 1920, 18 months after the Revolution, a purely bourgeois government was elected and the employers gained the upper hand. The many clauses of the Weimar Constitution that guaranteed women the legal and political equality for which Social Democracy had fought, remained mere scraps of paper because of the impotence of the working class movement and the chaotic state of the economy.

In order to assess the real position of women in the first years after the war and in the period of inflation, the fact that women were forced out of their jobs is much more crucial than the fact that they were granted formal equality. It was the organized workers themselves, feeling the pressure of the crisis, who were partly responsible. It showed that even when the women's movement had won women the right to work, to be protected in their work and to have equal status with men in law and politics, this was not enough to realize their emancipation, and that in times of economic crisis the rights they had already won would be lost once more.

> In drafting its legislation, the Government of the People's Representatives forgot that social reform is like an organism that cannot exist without air, and that its success is dependent upon the general economic situation. The most ideal social reforms are of no avail if the employer is not wealthy enough to support the cost; if the State is too poor to fulfil its social obligations; if the workman finds his wages rendered valueless in his hands by the swift progress of inflation; or, finally, if the political power in the State is seized by forces inimical to Labour that are able at will to pick holes in social legislation. The fate of social reform in

Germany depended in November, 1918, and the succeeding months upon that of German economy. Yet the Government achieved nothing whatever in the sphere of economic policy.[16]

It is difficult to provide statistical evidence to back up the complaints that women were being forced out of the production process in the first years after the war.[17] Statistics of the German Reich giving the number of unemployed together with the number of the population are available only for the years 1895 and 1925. For the post-war years, therefore, it is necessary to rely on statistics which were not primarily aimed at finding out the level of unemployment. They include, particularly,

1 statistics on the membership of sick funds,
2 statistics on the number of unemployed on the dole,
3 statistics on the number of trade-union members unemployed, and
4 statistics concerning the pressure felt by the offices of the Department of Employment.

Naturally, the general validity of conclusions drawn from such statistics can only be conditional, for any evaluation of the material which deviates from the original purpose of the enquiry must inevitably bring with it sources of error. Thus, for example, with regard to point 2, it was precisely the women who 'were not dependent on wages' who were dismissed, and they were therefore also not entitled to receive unemployment benefits. With regard to point 3, women made up only one-fifth of the membership of the trade unions, and the trade unions themselves only comprised a small section of the working class, and regarding point 4, in periods of crisis many of the unemployed had not even reported to the Department of Employment.

The available statistics thus only provide an indirect source of information about unemployment, but by making allowance for this we can derive the following picture for female unemployment from 1918 to 1924: In the demobilization crisis, the re-employment of the demobilized men resulted in an upward movement in the male membership curve for the sick funds, which contrasted with a manifest decline in the case of women. The emergency measures, forced employment and improvements in external trade relations, reduced male unemployment to a low ebb in 1920, while unemployment rose to over 5 per cent among women trade unionists. The number of women on the dole was higher in 1920 than in any of the three subsequent years. After a low point in 1922, there was a slight increase in the number of people on the dole before the onset of inflation and the Ruhr crisis. In 1924 the curve rose above the million mark. Of 1.2 million people on the dole, 577,567 were women, which was about half of the total, while their share in employment was only about one-third. Ten per cent of women trade unionists were unemployed, and 35 per cent were on short-time. The corresponding figures for male trade unionists were 10.2 per cent and 25 per cent respectively. Taking the annual average from 1919 to 1924, unemployment was greater among female than male trade union members. The proportions were even more pronounced in the case of workers partially laid off between 1921 and 1924. Added to this was the fact that women were rarely seasonal workers, who were only marginally affected by having to work short-time.

In the first post-war years, therefore, the employment of women not only declined, or female unemployment not only rose, but even in the industries primarily employing women (especially textiles, clothing and tobacco) they were affected more than their male counterparts by short-time work, that is, by a reduction of their daily working hours to avoid dismissals when business was poor. Despite the shortage of statistical material, there is thus evidence to support the claims made at Social Democratic Party Conferences and Women's Conferences in the post-war period that women were being forced out of the production process. As we shall seek to demonstrate in our discussion of female labour in the period of so-called 'stabilization', the increase in female unemployment after 1918 was not due solely to the return of female labour to its peace-time proportions. Rather, it persisted even after an increase in the number of workers began to show up after 1924, as a result, in its turn, of an increase in the population, inland migration, reductions in the armed forces, and the incorporation of domestic personnel, family people of private means and those formerly self-employed into the process of production.

b/Departure from the Old Theory of Emancipation

In order to understand the changes in the Social Democratic theory of women's emancipation after 1918, and the way in which it deviated from the line represented by Clara Zetkin, we must have

D

recourse to a discussion on women's emancipation which took place in the *Sozialistische Monatshefte* in 1905. The *Sozialistische Monatshefte* had been started in 1899, and its increasing importance lay in the fact that 'people who held views that could broadly be termed revisionist needed an organ in which they could publish their opinions without hindrance'.[18] The debate was sparked off by an article by Edmund Fischer, the most important sections of which deserve to be quoted, because they expressed the opposite of what had until then been regarded as valid within the Party. In his article, Fischer wrote:

> The real heart of the woman question is undoubtedly this: Is the unchangeable course of development leading to a situation where women generally will go out to work, and is this to be welcomed as a step forward because it will, in conjunction with the ensuing reorganization of the whole of social life, finally make woman free and economically independent of the male, thus making her emancipation a reality? Or is it unnatural, socially unhealthy, and harmful for women generally to work, a capitalist evil which will and must disappear with the abolition of capitalism?[19]

The first part of the alternative is completely in line with the views of the Marxist theorists, as described in the first section of this book and as they determined the party's line in the 1890s. The second part is typical of the views of the section of the working-class movement which remained caught in conservative ideals of the family and whose attitude to the woman question was consciously coloured by Proudhonism or was at least in agreement with the latter on this point.[20] Fischer left no doubt as to which of the two tendencies he supported:

> In my opinion, the old attitude to emancipation, which still lurks in the minds of many people, is no longer tenable today. Developments in female labour have not followed the direction assumed up till now, and state kitchens and household co-operatives are still utopian dreams that will always founder on the psychological nature of the human species, of women as well as of men.[21] The so-called emancipation of women goes against the nature of women and of mankind as a whole. It is unnatural, and hence impossible to achieve.[22]

Fischer thus sought to refute the theory proposed 'by Bebel, Kautsky, Zetkin and the others' with two arguments: the argument, on the one hand, of the facts of historical development, which differed from the prophesies, and on the other, of the facts of human nature.

It should be noted, firstly, that socialist theory did not by any means decree that all women should have jobs. It was considered a natural tendency of the capitalist economy, which would of course remain a 'capitalist evil' as long as the working-class movement failed to develop it into complete emancipation through the achievement of socialism. The trend towards greater independence for women, which was already becoming manifest in bourgeois society, was to be completed by socialism through the liberation of women from the constraint to work and through the defeat of the bourgeois ethic of work itself. The fact that the theory did not rely on a spontaneous transition from capitalist to socialist society to bring this about can be seen from the importance it attached to the revolutionary struggle of the working-class movement. Women industrial workers were to be drawn into this struggle by means of organization and political and economic education. Fischer's claim that developments in female labour had not 'followed the direction assumed up till now' is refuted by the fact that the number of women employed doubled between 1882 and 1925[23] and that until 1914 there was an upswing in the Social Democratic women's movement.

It was also a fact that the productive function of the family had been destroyed. The universalization of wage-labour meant that the family's role was reduced to consuming the wages earned by the working members. Female labour also abolished the traditional division of labour between the sexes. The social facilities which took over the socially useful work formerly done by women in the family did not, it is true, take the precise form of 'state kitchens and household cooperatives', but with dry-cleaning services, laundries, modern foodstores and homes, the use of machines for the mass production of cheap consumer goods and to facilitate housework, capitalist industry created the possibility for women to be liberated from the burdens of housework. Despite the potential surplus, it perpetuates both the constraint for women to find employment and the economically outmoded structure of the individual household. For capitalism, this is a reciprocal process: the need for independence which is drummed into the family for the purpose of increasing sales can generally be satisfied only if the wife goes out to work as well.

The historical development of female labour, which Fischer

seeks to use for his refutation of the socialist theory of women's emancipation, in fact only proves the accuracy of the thesis that the old family was being dissolved and that the social role of the woman was being changed by economic factors. The theory had never assumed this to be equivalent to the liberation of women. On the contrary, Clara Zetkin had pointed out that after women had been liberated from men they became socially dependent on capitalism and changed from domestic slaves into wage-slaves. Emancipation would only become a reality when this new dependence had also been abolished. Fischer, in contrast, could not imagine female labour as anything other than a capitalist phenomenon, and thus concluded that it needed to be abolished altogether. He built up a contradiction between the socialist goal of achieving free labour and his own demand to relieve women of more and more work.

The two demands were by no means contradictory, however. Socialism aimed, after all, to reduce work to its socially necessary level. By assuming that women's natural role was to be a mother and to bring up children, Fischer merely revived the old form of sexual slavery and overlooked the way in which the transformation of society also affected motherhood and the raising of children. Women's liberation was just as much a matter of having children brought up by society as it was of liberating women from unproductive housework and reducing their work to a socially necessary level. Fischer, however, imputed that its purpose was to reestablish an antiquated family situation with a traditional division of labour between the sexes, and rejected the opportunities and endeavours of women to change the social nature they had acquired under patriarchal conditions in the direction of greater independence not only from economic, but also from biological functions. The argument from the historical facts did not hold water, therefore, because Fischer gave the real tendencies a completely arbitrary interpretation in order to build up a contradiction between his own view and the socialist theory of women's emancipation.

Fischer's other argument, that human nature was constant, has been subjected to thorough criticism precisely by Marxist social theory.

Fischer thus not only dismissed the tendency for female labour to increase under capitalism and suggested that the contrary was true, but also expressed the desire for socialism to reverse, rather than complete, the emancipation which was already under way.

He failed to recognize the scope of the changes that had occurred in the family as a result of female labour and modern industry, and believed, in opposition to Clara Zetkin,[24] that socialism would in fact return the home and the family to its former status and enable them to resume the form that had been destroyed by capitalism.

Fischer looked to human nature, which he said would weather all social changes, as the principal support for his thesis. It is not difficult to show that his proof led him into all sorts of contradictions. He claimed, for example, that 'even after leaving school, the daughters of workers and country dwellers still enjoy exactly the same opportunities of development as the boys'.[25] The moulding of the female character, however, already begins in early childhood. The female modes of behaviour, which Fischer regards as an unchangeable part of nature, are very much socially determined. The social differentiation of the sexes does not by any means start only at the age of puberty. It is initiated in the very early stages of upbringing.[26] The fact that women's socially defined role later comes into conflict with their economic activity is a problem peculiar to modern capitalist development.

Although Fischer ignored this social aspect of women's nature and could thus only adduce biological facts to explain it, he claimed on the other hand, that the 'variety of intellectual life and capabilities' which emerged with puberty and motherhood 'did not in the least form an obstacle to women's emancipation and women's general independence in matters of work', and that the 'impediment to women's emancipation is found in another sphere'. According to Fischer, the crucial reason for the inevitable failure of women's emancipation was the fact that under capitalism nine-tenths of the women would be forced to work in factories and that they would therefore prefer to stay at home, unless they were nonetheless compelled to take a job because of their own or their family's distress.[27] Fischer did not foresee the changes that would take place in female labour, and obviously considered that factory work was the only work that women would be able to do under capitalism. Following the 'epoch of rationalization' in the German economy, however, women increasingly found employment in white collar jobs. And through the advances in workers' protection, accident prevention and social legislation, even factory work lost much of its former horror.

Besides this, Fischer ignored the changes that were taking place in the family itself, such as the increasing economy of work in the home, which tended precisely to free women from the traditional activities which Fischer declared to be the real domain of women. Not even the raising of children has been spared from this tendency. Fischer would probably have described this development as a 'capitalist evil' and assigned socialism the task of reversing it.

The line of argument with which Fischer tried to refute the feminist thesis of the oppression of women was not without its funny side. He wrote:

> There must be a few religious women who will let the brutality of their husbands stop them from going to church. But hundreds of thousands—if not millions—of men, allow their wives to stop them from living according to their political convictions or even let themselves be dragged off to church against all their beliefs. Men's dependence on women must thus be at least as great as vice versa.[28]

In his zeal to take the socialist theory of women's emancipation to the point of absurdity, Fischer missed the point that such a state of affairs, which was not disputed by the feminists, was the result of the very outmoded home situation which he was seeking to preserve as befitting women's nature. By rejecting as utopian all the measures suggested by the Socialists, such as large household co-operatives and state responsibility for the upkeep of children, Fischer left no other road open to himself than to assert the indestructability of the proven institutions of the individual household, the housewife and the nuclear family.

> Developments are not destroying the family of today, for it accords with man's whole nature . . . Any changes that the latter [the family—WT] will undergo as a result of the development of the relations of production, a higher culture, and socialism, can only consist of the fact that women will have a number of their jobs taken from them, or that these jobs will be made easier . . . It will then be shown that women's primary and highest aim in life, which is deeply embedded in their nature as a woman, is: to be mothers, and to live for the care and raising of children, while as a rule only unmarried women want to have economic independence.[29]

Fischer does not make clear how he manages to reconcile the increasing tendency for women to be relieved of jobs with 'women's aim in life, deeply embedded in their nature as a woman', 'to be mothers, and to live for the care and raising of children'.

It is true that wage-labour under capitalist conditions 'cannot enrich women's lives more than housework can', but the socialist theory had not expected anything different. On the contrary, it envisaged that the experience of wage-labour would bring women to oppose society as it was, while housework prevented them from participating in political conflicts. In the last resort, Fischer was not concerned to preserve women from the misery of factory work at all, nor was he interested in seeing them overcome their oppression under patriarchism. He only desired to enable them to pursue their 'natural occupation' unhindered. Women should not work, even in socialist society, because this was in contradiction to their nature; however, work in the home could not absorb them fully either, partly because social institutions were taking over some of its functions, and partly because it was being mechanized.

Even children were only brought up at home for the first few years, so that their upbringing could not constitute women's 'natural role' either, unless Fischer envisaged a process of unbroken motherhood, with the birth of another child as soon as the previous one had outgrown its mother. That can hardly be said to have anything in common with the liberation of women. The real aim of the socialist emancipation of women, which was to create freedom through the lapse of traditional constraints, thus fails to appear at all in Fischer's articles. He merely transformed women's biological nature, and brushed aside the fact that she was subjugated to the purpose of preserving the species by asserting that only unmarried women wanted economic independence. He thus admitted, it is true, that such economic independence disappeared upon marriage, but at the same time he postulated that motherhood reconciled women to the dependence of their existence. The question as to whether this was desirable or not is ruled out from the start by the allegation that it is women's natural role to be a housewife and mother.

Fischer's entire investigation thus inevitably came to the conclusion:

> The idea of all women having jobs, being completely independent economically from the male, and hence that society should take over full responsibility for the care and upbringing of children and individual households and the family should be dissolved, is a dream—and not a pretty one by any means!—left over from the infancy of the socialist movement.[30]

The trade unionists of the 1860s and 1870s had rejected female labour because they thought it better for women to be kept out of work under the conditions of the time, but they supported female labour under different social conditions. Fischer, in contrast, did not even consider the idea that working conditions could change, and asserted that female labour was incompatible with women's nature, thus brushing aside emancipation as a 'utopian dream'. In the same way as other critics of socialist 'utopias', Fischer was unable to project contemporary developments and imagine fundamental social and human characteristics different from those of the present. At best he was still able to recognize their emergence, but he could not cast doubt on their absolute validity. Fischer's reservations concerning the theory of emancipation were in part thoroughly warranted—his idea, for example, that the home and family sphere was preferable to the alienated world of industrial labour—or that the men were likewise victims of the domestic slavery to which they condemned the women. The essential points of Fischer's refutation, however, revealed an inadequate understanding of socialist theory and a tendency to make absolute precisely those social conditions that were predominant in his time.

Fischer's essays provoked a flood of articles against him. Clara Zetkin wrote a very sharp reply in *Die Gleichheit*.[31] The *Sozialistische Monatshefte* likewise published numerous contributions refuting Fischer's apodictic conclusions or individual aspects of his articles, including replies, for example, by Emma Ihrer, Oda Olberg, Adams-Lehmann and Wally Zepler.[32]

Even though Fischer's articles did not escape contradiction by the female theorists, the mere fact of their publication can nonetheless be taken as a symptom of the approaching revision of the old theory of women's emancipation. As Social Democracy was restructured, Fischer's new formulation of the woman question gained in importance along with the revision of economic and political theories. In 1917, the *Sozialistische Monatshefte* published an unprecedented number of articles on female labour in war-time. Among them was a discussion by Fischer of the 'tendencies of female labour', in which he reinforced his 1905 thesis. He predicted that the tendency which he had at that time described as natural would win through:

The increase in the number of married women workers during the war and probably in the immediate post-war period can thus only signify a time of serious distress, while their increasing prosperity thereafter must cause the same tendencies to reappear as were evident before the war: a movement towards the disappearance of wage-labour for married women, since wage-labour cannot enrich their lives more than housework can. It is a burden and reduces the enjoyment of life.[33]

The error of this prediction derives from the fact that Fischer makes a false assumption as to the relation between economic depression and the increase in female labour, or between economic prosperity and its decline. If we look at individual cases, the constraint in individual families for women to go out and work will obviously decrease as the husband's income rises, while on the other hand a small family income will increase the pressure on women to take a job. If we look at the German economy after the First World War, however, we see that there was a decline in the employment of women in the period of crisis, and an increase in the period of economic prosperity. Admittedly, this phenomenon was not caused by the policy of the employers, but by the mandatory measures of the state and the pressure of male trade unionists, who always preferred an unemployed woman to an unemployed man. We can ignore the origins, however, in view of the manifest fact that developments in Germany after 1924 refuted Fischer's thesis that female labour would decline as social prosperity increased.

In 1917, in contrast to 1905, there was hardly any protest at Fischer's views; the numerous articles which appeared in the *Sozialistische Monatshefte* concentrated exclusively on the practical problems of female labour, such as its connexion with women's interest in politics, the protection of women workers, the situation of women in individual branches of industry, and the like.

In 1919, Wally Zepler published a book called *Sozialismus und Frauenfrage (Socialism and the Woman Question)*, which brought together Fischer's article from the *Sozialistische Monatshefte* of 1905 and a reply by Oda Oldberg, 'Polemics on the Woman Question and Socialism', which had appeared in the same journal, as well as personal contributions which had likewise partly been published in the *Sozialistische Monatshefte*. Although Wally Zepler was not exactly on the left of the Party, as is evidenced by the comments we have quoted by her on the contribution of Social Democracy to the education of soldiers, she criticized Fischer's position. She objected above all to his argument that the majority of women found housework preferable to a job, accusing him of drawing conclusions about 'the average attitude of the future generation from the inclinations, feelings and desires of the intellectually untrained and predominantly undifferentiated average proletariat woman of today'.[34] The reason why women were as Fischer described them, she said, was that they 'lacked the energy to think or live' and that 'the seeds which would enable them to form their own views and lives were dried up by the women's need to accommodate themselves to the male circle of life and ideas'.[35] The exertion of strength demanded by motherhood would inevitably reduce women's opportunities as long as its effect was to lessen their ability to compete with the male. Only when society had also given material recognition to motherhood as a social service and taken an increasing responsibility for children's up-bringing would the women be able to achieve equal status with men even during maternity, and subsequently through their own work.[36]

After the appearance of Wally Zepler's book there was no further discussion on the socialist theory of women's emancipation until the years of mass unemployment. It is typical that her book offered no analysis of female labour and women's liberation after the Revolution and reverted instead to the state of the discussion in 1905. Admittedly the most important tenets of the old theory were retained, but there was no attempt to apply them to the new situation. After the dismissal of Clara Zetkin as the editor of *Die Gleichheit*, Luise Zietz's exclusion from the Party executive, and the split in the Party and the women's movement, Wally Zepler's book did not form the prelude to a new theoretical discussion but was a mere sequel to a development that had led to a political separation from the supporters of radical women's emancipation and to the revision of their theory.

The minutes of the Social Democratic Party Conference and Women's Conferences show that Fischer's reaction against the theory of women's emancipation was not an isolated instance, but a symptom of the theory's decline. It is true that the old theory was no longer attacked formally, but it was undermined directly by the Party's policy and indirectly by the effect that this had on the Party and on society.

7/The Women's Question at Conferences of the Party and the Women's Movement

a/The Görlitz (1921) and Heidelberg (1925) Party Programmes

At the first Party Conference after the War, and at the adjoining Women's Conference (in Weimar, in 1919), Marie Juchacz presented a very disillusioning report on women's involvement in parliamentarism, and Gertrud Hanna spoke of the consequences for women of the so-called 'transitional economy'.[1] They failed to draw the conclusion, however, that the achievement of female suffrage had not brought a decisive step forward in the emancipation of women.

At the following Party Conference (Kassel, 1920) it was already made clear that there had been a substantial deterioration in the situation of women workers since the end of the war.[2]

In 1921, the Görlitz Party Conference adopted a new programme, which included a number of the principles and demands of women's emancipation and protection: the fight for complete constitutional and practical equality for all citizens over 20 years of age, with no distinction as to sex, origin, and religion, and for the involvement of women in all judiciary offices; combined education for and by both sexes; the prohibition of night work for women, and their prohibition from working in enterprises particularly detrimental to health or at machines where there was a particularly high accident risk, and the proclamation of women's universal right to work.[3]

The Heidelberg programme of 1925 reiterated the principles of women's right to work and co-education. It did not contain any special clauses about the protection of women, but it did demand this time, that the constitutional equality of all citizens should should be put into effect and it repeated the demand that women be given equal status with men in civil law.[4] The organizational section of the constitution laid down that women members were to be given representation on the committees of all organizations and on all delegations in proportion to their numbers, and provision was made for lower membership fees for female members. At least two women were to be on the Party's executive, and the number of female members needed to send a representative into the Party Committee was reduced to 75,000.[5]

Starting from the Görlitz Party Conference, discussion on questions affecting women at Social Democratic Congresses centred on a series of constantly recurring themes: the distribution of women's votes over the various parties, the number of women Party members, criticism of the women's papers, the discrimination against women in the Party, and the importance of women's involvement in social work. Until the Leipzig Party Conference in 1931 there were no further signs of any investigation into the contradiction that existed between capitalist relations of production and the emancipation of women, which had been the primary concern of the women's movement in Clara Zetkin's time.

b/The Women's Vote in Elections

The 1918 Revolution gave women universal, equal, active and passive suffrage, as had been demanded in the programme of Social Democracy since 1891.[6]

The electoral code also made provision for men and women to vote separately, which was essential to assess the patterns of female voting. It was only implemented sporadically and irregularly, however,[7] so that for a long time the discussion on female voting had no objective data on which to base itself.

The Social Democratic Party never had an overwhelming victory at the polls, and it seemed obvious to ask whether it was the women who were responsible for this. Throughout the Weimar period there was a vehement discussion on the way women had voted. The men were disappointed that by giving women the suffrage the Party had to a certain extent put an instrument in the hands of the reactionary forces. It was very tempting to blame the Party's defeat in June 1920 on the women. It was the most obvious means of defence against an investigation into the reasons for the failure of the Revolution.

It is open to question, however, whether the male members of the Party had in fact expected women's suffrage to bring victory to the Socialists. Even the adherents of women's emancipation were under no illusions about the forces that primarily influenced the women's vote. For the opponents of female suffrage, the outcome of the elections confirmed their worst fears. Thus women's suffrage did not mean a further step within the Party towards the elimination of antagonism between the sexes, but intensified it. After the National Assembly elections, which were the first in which women were able to take part, the *Gewerkschaftliche Frauenzeitung* wrote that Social Democracy would probably have obtained an absolute majority if there had not been female suffrage.[8] Anna Blos expressed similar thoughts in *Die Gleichheit*.[9] At the Görlitz Party Conference in 1921, the report on the women's movement was very cautious:

> Statistics show that numerically speaking there was strong female participation in the elections, but partial assessments suggest that women's suffrage has not yet been very favourable to Social Democracy.[10]

There was a great scarcity of statistical data on which to base an assessment of women's voting, however. Men and women had voted separately in a few cities only. But these few results were sufficient to feed the anti-feminist's prejudices, while the Social Democratic women attempted to explain the election results in terms of women's lack of independence, which was a result of their former oppression and which drove them into the arms of the conservative parties. At the Görlitz Party Conference of 1921 it was said:

> We women are accused of not having used our votes correctly. Big brother is calling little sister names. If there had been more practical socialism in families in the thirty years that we were able to carry on our work unhindered, then the women would also have had a much greater love and understanding of socialism and would have made better use of the votes which the Revolution gave them. . . . It is the big brother who is to blame. Formerly, women were not considered worthy of education, and now we must all suffer as a result.[11]

The phrase 'practical socialism in the family' no doubt referred to the fact that men ought to have abandoned their patriarchal attitudes and behaviour and treated their wives as equals. Marx, Engels, and Bebel, of course, had been convinced that in proletarian families the old male privileges had been deprived of their material basis. But where there was a sexual division of labour between the productive male, who maintained his family, and the housewife who simply prepared, conserved and consumed, there was ample support for men's resistance against the acknowledgement of female parity. The demand for the 'socialization of the family' placed the responsibility for women's emancipation on the husbands and substituted the idea of men enlightening the women for the emancipation of society. Admittedly, many workers were aware of the equal value of women's services in the home. But this attitude did not break through the illusory nature of the productivity of the housewife, which was only maintained through the backwardness of their households behind what was technologically and socially possible. If such possibilities were fully exhausted, the waste of energy perpetuated in the home would inevitably have become obvious very quickly.

At the SPD's National Women's Conference in Berlin in 1924, which was devoted entirely to the theme of 'Women and Elections', Marie Juchacz likewise came to the conclusion that the women had failed, i.e. had not voted for the right party.[12] The evidence to support such assertions was highly inadequate, however. As the first criterion for 'correct' voting, it would have been necessary to juxtapose the votes of male and female workers for Social Democracy and the other parties. A comparison could then have been made between the men in occupations that were particularly inclined to Social Democracy, and the women in these occupations. Only a comparable socio-economic situation would have permitted tenable conclusions to be drawn about the political behaviour of the respective sexes.

Apart from the economic situation, an analysis of the way in which wives of Social Democratic voters and Party members had voted could have given an indication of the women's party preferences. Only such comparisons could really do justice to the women's voting behaviour, but the statistical material for them was unavailable. A simple comparison of male and female votes showed in fact that the percentage of women who had voted for Social Democracy was smaller than that of the men. It is not known what information provided the basis for the judgement passed at the Görlitz Party Conference in 1921 concerning women's votes for the German Nationalist Party. It was said that

They are women who by their class situation belong to Social Democracy—wives of civil servants, wives of the so-called middle class, wives of the petty bourgeoisie, domestic workers, women and girls who work in offices and shops, who are employed in sewing or other workshops, or in factories.[13]

If Social Democracy was regarded as the Party that represented the interests of wage-dependent workers and thus of the overwhelming part of the population, then it may have seemed paradoxical that there were workers who voted for the bourgeois parties. On the one hand, however, the wage-dependent workers did not form a homogeneous body, but were differentiated in many ways according to types and levels of income, status in the production process and political ideology; class status and class consciousness need not coincide, and there had never been a united front of all wage-dependent workers. The relationship of Social Democracy to the 'so-called middle class' presented even greater difficulties. Although the number of small independent traders declined in times of depression and they suffered from the competition of large-scale industry, this by no means resulted in a tendency for them to vote for Social Democracy.

On the other hand, the Party had itself to blame for the departure of countless voters after 1919. In 1919 the Social Democrats had managed to win 45 per cent of all voters to their side. The election defeat in June 1920 was a reaction to the Party's inability and unwillingness to take seriously the social revolution which they had promised and for which many hoped. The vote of confidence which Social Democracy had been given to transform society in line with its principles was squandered on the government's campaign against the rebellious workers and lost through its toleration and use of counter-revolutionary military groups and ministerial bureaucrats, and the caution with which the Party believed it had to proceed. The effects of the peace treaty and the advancing devaluation of money were making themselves felt. The Social Democrats, as Marie Juchacz said at the Görlitz Party Conference in 1921, had:

promised peace and bread, and within the framework of the possible they have also kept all their promises, but a large section of the women that joined the Party purely on the strength of their emotions amidst the turbulence of the revolutionary atmosphere felt cheated of their hopes, for they had not had any political education.[14]

The 'framework of the possible' which is here mentioned was constructed by the Party itself, for it had shrunk back from a decisive socialist policy. After the Party had in various ways shown the various social classes that it was not serious about the revolution, it was useless for it now to tell the workers that 'by their class status' they ought to retain their confidence in the SPD. The grand bourgeoisie wanted a Restoration anyhow, the middle strata suffered serious financial setbacks under the economic conditions of the time, and the radical workers were squashed. Under such circumstances it was a symptom of self-righteousness to accuse the women of not having made the correct use of their vote. Marie Juchacz gave an accurate assessment of the voters' feelings at the Berlin National Women's Conference in 1924. No one, she said, had been satisfied with the election results. This was because

> the women have been tired out by the bad state of the economy and only feel instinctively that it was better before. It is because they do not ask why this is so that they incline towards the right to such an extent.[15]

On the other side it was said that in times of economic distress women were more easily influenced than men by the agitation of the extremist parties.[16] In the first place, it must be stressed that election statistics offer no support for the assertion that women were particularly susceptible to political extremism. Up till 1930, the 'extremist' parties of the Weimar period, which were generally taken to be the National Socialist and Communist Parties, enjoyed less support from women than from men. They were decidedly 'male parties'.[17]

But even if it had been possible to adduce proof for the thesis of women's susceptibility to political 'extremism', this would only have underlined the fact that they felt the shortcomings of the new republic too clearly in the form of inflation, rising food prices and unemployment, to be able to have confidence in the Socialist or Republican parties who were responsible for this Republic. This might have been regarded as evidence of inadequate political education, and it may be argued in retrospect that the Weimar Regime would not have come to such a sorry end if the women had not withdrawn their confidence from it. In actual fact, the distress of the early twenties was stronger than any political propaganda, and it is pointless to accuse the women of drawing the wrong conclusions from their misery.

In 1921 *Die Neue Zeit* tried for the first time, using statistical material, to reach a definitive judgment on women's voting. The results of the first Reichstag elections in the cities of Hasbach/ Schwarzwald, Cologne and Hanover were investigated, and they showed that:

> The anti-democratic and anti-republic parties do in fact owe their rise in a large measure to the women. In 1919, when they were still feeling the effects of the war, many women voted for the Social Democrats solely because it was they who had given them the vote; this time, however, they have voted, often for economic reasons, against the Socialist parties.

Die Gesellschaft (Society), the new scientific journal of Social Democracy as from 1924, published a thorough study of women's electoral behaviour by Max Schneider.[18] Schneider starts from the assertion, 'not all that rarely heard among Socialists', that even the 1919 elections to the National Assembly would have produced a Socialist majority if the men had voted alone. Since, however, 'separate voting for men and women only took place in very few German constituencies, it is hardly possible to prove this claim'. Schneider bases his study on the election results from the city of Cologne. The preconditions for an analysis were particularly favourable there, for separate voting had taken place in all elections since 1919.

In the first instance Schneider demonstrates the women's greater disappointment or 'change of mood' as compared with the men by reference to the fluctuations in their turnout for the elections. A consideration of the distribution of votes over the individual parties in Cologne reveals the same picture:

> In the elections for the National Assembly, the Socialist Parties received 48.1 per cent of the male, and 33.1 per cent of the female votes, making about 40 per cent all told. In the first Reichstag election, they obtained 45.8 per cent of the male, and 29.9 per cent of the female votes, a total of 39.1 per cent, and in the second Reichstag election 37.7 per cent of the male votes, 23.2 per cent of the female, or 30.8 per cent altogether. In the third Reichstag election, 39.9 per cent of the men, and 24.4 per cent of the women, a total of 32.2 per cent, voted for them.

These results show that despite the strong influence of the Church in Cologne, a third of the women voters initially gave their support to the Socialists, and thus made correct use, from the standpoint of Social Democracy, of the suffrage which they had only just been granted. After this, however, more women than men were disappointed, and they partially returned to the 'large camp of the non-voters' or turned to other political parties.

Schneider is far from accusing the women of 'failure' for this reason. Rather he seems inclined to see the fact that a third of the women had voted for Social Democracy in Cologne, despite the influence of the Church and the Centre, as a sign of the women's progressiveness. He says:

> What a long time it took for a third of the male voters to become so well educated as to vote for the Social Democrats. In the elections of 1912, which was the most successful for Social Democracy before the War, 34.8 of every 100 valid votes were cast for Social Democracy. The first Reichstag election took place in 1871. It thus took Social Democracy thirty years to obtain a third of the votes.

If the comments by Social Democrats concerning women's electoral behaviour are combined with the results of a study published by Gabriele Bremme, which gives an assessment of all the material on separate voting in the Weimar period, we obtain the following picture: in all the elections, the female turnout was less than the male.[19] It is impossible to speak of a 'cyclical' pattern for female abstention. By this is meant the fact that 'the recurrent struggle between the parties for political power only aroused women's interest . . . when it involved fundamental political decisions affecting basic questions concerning the state or the social order and hence women's own personal fate.'[20] A study of the women's party preferences shows that there was a drop in their votes for Social Democracy after 1919, which must be attributed to the fact that their hopes were disappointed. As from 1928, there is a renewed growth in women's votes for Social Democracy, but as from 1930 this contrasts with an ever more significant increase in their votes for the right-wing parties.[21] Neither the SPD's friendly attitude towards women, nor the National Socialists' marked hostility to women's involvement in politics, influenced women's voting as such.[22]

Even though married women turned out in greater numbers

than single ones at elections,[23] which points to the fact that the influence of work on arousing political interest must not be over-estimated, the election turnout among women members of some qualified occupations (civil servants, self-employed people and people in free occupations) was higher than that of the married women and was largely equivalent to that of the male members of these occupational groups, or, as in the case of female civil servants, even higher than that of their male counterparts.[24] While the women's election turnout and also their share of votes for the individual parties never reached that of the men, the Centre, alone among all the parties, revealed a percentage of women's votes which was constantly above that of the men.[25] After fourteen years of women's electoral practice, the Social Democrats were forced to note that the introduction of women's suffrage had not only altered the relationship of power to their advantage, but that, on the contrary, the majority of the women's votes had gone to the con-servative and even the reactionary parties. If the question of guilt is to be raised at all, then the women can only be blamed for the limited success or defeat of Social Democracy in the case of the National Assembly elections and those for the first Reichstag. It was precisely the first election, however, which had mobilized the largest percentage of women for Social Democracy, a figure that was never again reached. The decline in women's votes for the Socialists in later years must hence be seen in the context of the shift in the political relationship of power and the economic situation as a whole. In view of these developments, to say that women had a fundamentally conservative attitude seems to miss the point.

Nonetheless, the fact that they were so quick to withdraw their confidence from Social Democracy may in actual fact have been due to their lack of political education. The women them-selves were not to blame for this, however, and Max Schneider was right to point to the fact that forty years of preparation were required to win a third of the male voters over to Social Democracy.

The vexed question as to whether women's suffrage brought benefits to the Party must thus be answered in the negative, but it must be added in the interests of fairness that the circumstances which led women to give so little support to the Party or turned them away from it were due partly to the social oppression and intellectual dependence of the women, which was a legacy from the past that had not been overcome in the present, and partly to the failure to bring about a social transformation after 1918.

Table 2

Survey of the fluctuation of female SPD membership.[26]

Year	Party members	Female Party members	Per cent women	Absolute change from previous year
1906	384,327[a]	6,460[i]	1.7	+2,460
1907	530,446[a]	10,943[j]	2.1	+4,483
1908	527,336[a]	29,458[j]	5.6	+18,515
1909	633,309[a]	62,259[j]	9.8	+32,801
1910	720,038[a]	82,642[k]	11.5	+20,383
1911	836,562[a]	107,693[k]	12.9	+25,051
1912	970,112[a]	130,371[k]	13.4	+22,678
1913	982,850[a]	141,115[k]	14.4	+10,744
1914	1,085,905[a]	174,751[l]	16.1	+33,639
1915	515,898[a]	?	?	?
1916	432,618[a]	107,336[l]	24.8	−67,418
1917	243,061[a]	66,608[m]	27.4	−40,728
1918	249,411[a]	70,659[m]	28.3	−4,059
1919	1,012,299[a]	206,354[m]	20.4	+135,695
1920	1,180,208[a]	207,000[a]	17.5	+646
1921	1,221,059[a]	192,485[a]	15.8	−11,522
1922	1,174,105[b]	?	?	?
1923	1,261,072[b]	130,000[b]	10.3	−62,485
1924	940,078[c]	148,125[c]	15.8	+18,125
1925	844,495[c]	152,693[c]	18.1	+5,568
1926	823,520[d]	165,492[d]	20.1	+11,799
1927	866,671[e]	181,541[e]	20.9	+16,049
1928	937,381[f]	198,771[f]	21.2	+17,230
1929	949,306[f]	201,000[f]	21.2	+2,229
1930	1,037,384[g]	228,278[g]	22.0	+27,278
1931	1,008,953[h]	230,331[h]	22.8	+2,053

c/The Fluctuation in the Proportion of Female Party Members

A study of the membership curve from 1906 shows that the greatest increase in the number of female members occurred after the abolition of the old Combination Laws, from 1908 to 1914 and then in 1920 and from 1925 to 1928 (see Table 2). From 1906 to 1920 female membership rose from 6,460 to 207,000. This 1920 peak was not surpassed until 1931, with 230,331 women members. The number of female members reached its lowest ebb in 1923, while that of the men did not do so until 1925, following the stabilization of the economy. There was a rapid decline in female membership from 1920 to 1923, and then a steady increase from 1924 to 1931. The male membership, in contrast, rose in the period of inflation (1920–1923). Stabilization was followed by a downward rush in the number of male members, from which the Party did not completely recover until 1931.

The men thus reacted to the economic crisis by joining the Party in increasing numbers, while the women responded with an increasing exodus. Conversely, stabilization in 1924 was followed by a greater intake of women into the Party, while the men turned their backs on it.

This movement is reflected in the percentage of female Party members. Before the War, it reached 16 per cent in 1914, when the total strength of the Party was 1,085,905. Sixteen years later, in 1930, when the Party had almost the same number of members, it was 22 per cent. Between 1920 and 1931 the women's share fluctuated from 10.3 per cent (1923) to 22 per cent. This was due principally to the exodus of male members (especially after 1923), but also to movements within the female membership. We have already drawn one conclusion from the fluctuations of the number of women in the SPD: the women left the Party during the War years. The fact that, as a result of the demobilization decrees, women suffered the highest unemployment in these years, suggests that there is a connexion between Party membership and employment, or Party exodus and unemployment in the case of women. The fact that such a connexion did exist was underlined by developments in the years following stabilization. Marie Juchacz seems to have sought a similar explanation when she said:

> My own observations suggest that work is a training ground for political life, while restriction to the narrow confines of the household results in narrowmindedness and the suppression of class consciousness. The lack of education through work also makes itself felt in the decline of our membership figures.[27]

Marie Juchacz's optimistic forecasts concerning women's involvement in the Party once the crisis was overcome[28] were not

fulfilled, however. There was no substantial increase beyond the
high-point before 1920.

At the beginning of the 1920s it was suggested that to con-
solidate the level of female membership 'circles of specialists and
interested men and women' should be set up 'to try and find out
for once the economic and psychological reasons for the decline
in female membership and to work out ways of countering it'.[29] It
was also said that the manner in which women in other countries
were asked to attend to general matters more than to those particularly affecting them was worthy of emulation. A few years later,
in contrast, there was advocacy of 'women's evenings, women's
leisure groups and evenings concerned with the women's world'.[30]
Unemployment, inflation and the working-class movement's loss of
power did not enable the women's movement to reach a clear line
in its agitation. It was the 'fantastic situation' in which 'dissatisfaction with capital mismanagement, . . . weakened the Parties of
the Left and gave an increased following to those of the right'.[31]

d / The Debate on the Press

The disappearance of female members inevitably led people to
ask whether or not the Party was employing the right tactics as far
as women were concerned. The Party could not abolish unemployment, which was considered to be the real cause of the decline of
the women's movement, any more than it could abolish capitalism.
This fatal connexion completely dominated the working-class
movement. The Party had come to hold local and governmental
responsibility in many spheres and it now had to find ways of re-
taining such positions. It therefore concentrated its efforts on
winning new supporters. Methods of political propaganda thus
obtained particular significance.

In the women's movement, the debate on effective agitation
centred on the movement's publications. The few facts that can
be gleaned from the proceedings of Party and women's conferences,
and from the periodicals themselves (see Table 3), give the following, unfortunately very incomplete, picture of the state of the
women's movement's papers:

Table 3

Survey of the circulation of Social Democratic women's magazines between 1913 and 1931.[32]

Name of paper		Date	Circulation
Die Gleichheit (1891 to 1922)		1913	112,000[a]
„	July	1914	124,000[b]
„	December	1914	58,000[b]
„		1915	46,500[b]
„		1916	35,500[b]
„		1917	19,000[b]
„		1918	28,000[b]
„	May	1919	33,000[b]
„	Nov	1920	11,000[c]
„	March	1921	20,500[c]
„	September	1921	25,000[c]
Gewerkschaftliche Frauenzeitung (1916 till *c.* 1933)		1917	100,000[d]
Die Kämpferin (Women's paper of the USPD until 1922)		1922	38,500[e]
Die Frauenwelt (1924 to 1933)	1st half year	1924	67,000[f]
„	2nd half year	1924	90,000[g]
„	end	1925	*c* 100,000[h]
Die Genossin (Information paper for female SPD officials)		1925	12,000[g]
„		1928	30,000[i]
„		1931	40,000[j]

The decline in the circulation of *Die Gleichheit* from 1913 to 1920, which was offset either quantitatively or qualitatively by any other women's magazine, was symptomatic of the decay of the women's movement. Clara Bohm-Schuch took over the editorship in 1921. *Die Gleichheit* was henceforth described as a 'magazine for the women of the German Social Democratic Party'. However, circulation was not increased by restricting the readership in this manner. Only about one Social Democratic woman in ten subscribed to *Die Gleichheit*, while in 1912, in contrast, nearly every female Party member had also been a subscriber to the magazine. There was a desire, however, to distance *Die Gleichheit* as clearly as possible from Clara Zetkin, who had given it the subtitle 'magazine for the interests of women workers'. Marie Juchacz described Clara Bohm-Schuch as a woman 'with a gift for poetic expression'[33] and under her leadership *Die Gleichheit*, despite the ambitious claims of its new title, increasingly became a family paper. The political articles lost their bite, and even though there were more men than previously among the contributors, a ghastly 'feminine' tone spread through the supplements. The subtitle was altered once more. As from 1922 it read: 'Magazine for women and girls of the working people, Organ of the United SPD'.

But not even the 'new course' was able to save *Die Gleichheit* from ruin. As from June 1919, it is true, it came out weekly, but the frequency of publication soon had to be reduced and limitations placed on the size of the paper. Even then, the magazine could only be kept going through substantial subsidies from the Party Executive. At the Görlitz Party Conference 25,000 subscribers could 'pleasingly' still be counted.[34] *Die Gleichheit* ceased publication in the autumn of 1922. Marie Juchacz writes that the Party Executive had resolved to try out a different type of paper.[35]

> Needless to say, the women's movement, too, had suffered severely in the period of inflation. The increase in female members which resulted from Unification [between the SPD and the USPD in September 1922—WT] was thus wiped out once more.
> *Die Gleichheit*, which had to be abandoned in this difficult period, also reappeared in a completely different guise, under the new name of *Die Frauenwelt (Women's World)*. Its success gives us reason to have the most pleasant hopes.[36]

These 'most pleasant hopes' were disappointed however. The origin of the new paper was ascribed alternately to the effects of inflation and to a dislike of the tradition of *Die Gleichheit*. It was already severely criticized at the National Women's Conference in 1924. *Die Frauenwelt* had the character of a leisure paper. So well was its political tendency hidden beneath the supplement, edifying stories, patterns and fashion illustration, that no one could rightly discover it any more. This disguise was seen as the product of great skill in line with the latest developments in the science of propaganda.

Die Genossin, on the other hand, existed purely to provide information for female Party officials. It published reports on marital law, the penal code, female labour, protection for women workers, the census of employment, movements of population, the illegitimacy law, protection for young people, local politics, matters concerning housewives, social hygiene, women's work in parliament, biographies, reports from the bourgeois and international women's movements, and book reviews.[37]

The changes in the women's movement's papers were not due solely to the effects of inflation, but also, as Marie Juchacz explained, to a deliberate policy decision. The new situation, she said, required a particular adaptation of propaganda, and *Die Frauenwelt* had therefore been set up in order to get to the masses of women who were politically apathetic. *Die Genossin* served to instruct female Party officials, and it offered all the material needed by the women in the Party for their work.[38] The women who disagreed with the Party executive's new formula for the women's papers rejected *Die Frauenzeitung* and demanded that *Die Gleichheit* be revived or that

> the scope of *Die Genossin* be widened to include, besides technical information for women officials, discussion of fundamental questions as well, for otherwise the women's movement will become shallow or submerged in everyday politics. Under no circumstances must the intellectualist education towards socialism suffer.[39]

The very clumsy demand for 'intellectualist education towards socialism' was in fact the alternative to the Party executive's allegedly scientific policy for the press. The people who were dissatisfied were trying to express at the Conference the fact that the dubious procedure of dressing up a socialist women's magazine to look like a bourgeois leisure paper would not win the Party new members. This could not be achieved by means of a disguise, but only by consistently educating women in the theory of scientific socialism. They were able to point out that the allegedly massive propaganda effect of *Die Frauenwelt* had failed to eventuate, and that in Berlin, for example, the readership of *Die Gleichheit* was identical with the female Party membership. Thus the very women that this magazine was meant to win for the Party were not even reading it. A minority repeatedly pointed to *Die Gleichheit* as a model:

> Our women comrades have not yet forgotten the fact that *Die Gleichheit*, as it used to be, contributed a great deal, if not everything, to the fact that women socialists were educated at all. We

hope that *Die Genossin* will at least compensate by half for *Die Gleichheit*, which is so painfully missed.[40]

Exception was also taken to the fact that the editor of *Frauenwelt* was a man, Dr Lohmann. But he was replaced by Mrs Toni Sender at the express demand of the Kiel Women's Conference only in 1927.[41] At the same conference, Marie Juchacz felt it necessary, in view of the severe criticism and the proposed resolution demanding the revival of *Die Gleichheit*, to make a statement about the Party executive's policy on the press. In order to fend off criticism, she first asked the critics what they thought of the material made available by the women's magazines. Clearly she meant to show the women once more that all their needs were taken care of. Juchacz pointed out that the women's legal status had changed and advised them to read the daily papers in order to get their orientation on the political situation. For everything else, *Die Genossin* was adequate. Genuine suggestions would always be welcomed. Up till now, however, there had not been any justified criticism. At the same time, however, it was conceded that no solution had yet been found to the problem of recruiting women workers.[42]

Criticism of the Party executive's press policy always met the same fate. The response partly took the form of intimidation, and partly found expression in pseudo-scientific evasions about the requirements of propaganda.

At the Berlin Women's Conference in 1924, for example, a woman demanded that *Die Frauenwelt* should deal a little with the real distress of women workers' lives, whereupon she had to let herself be told by the editor, Dr Lohmann:

> My own opinion on this matter, at any rate, and I know that I am supported here by the majority of women comrades in distress, who have emphasized the same to me in a whole series of letters, is that they do not want to have the misery of their domestic life before their eyes even in their leisure time. They want to be shown the sun which some day in the future will shine into their lives because of socialism.[43]

Without any embarrassment whatsoever, a representative of the Party bureaucracy could here stand up before an acquiescent majority and ward off critical ideas with clichés that anticipated those later used by the culture industry for the very same reason.

Having failed to change the world, the Party was now to

provide women with edifying literature, and the 'sun of socialism' would best shine 'some day in the future'. Critical attention to women's living conditions was cut short by the statement that oppressed women did not need literature that reproduced their own misery, but literature that edified and reconciled them with reality.

The women who proposed the resolution to revive *Die Gleichheit* had the new formula for the women's press held up to them. The critics were told that comrade Juchacz's address would no doubt have made all those who had voiced such 'bitter criticism' of *Die Frauenwelt* realize their mistake. And in case they still persisted in the belief that their objections were valid, it was disparagingly added that: 'It is not a question of what is wanted by individuals, but what is needed by the broad masses.'[44] Here again was an early form of the subsequently familiar argument of the culture industry, which justified the poor taste of its products by reference to the alleged desires of the consumer. It was certainly quite new for Social Democracy to allow the level of its publications to be prescribed by the most backward section of the population. Where pedagogical and even revolutionary goals had formerly held sway, policy was now dictated by the fear of shocking people with too crude an appearance, and by moderation in the dose of socialism.

> If people outside already described *Die Frauenwelt* as absolutely socialist, it would make our work much harder. We must have a paper that fulfils the purpose of gradual enlightenment and which does not have doors shut in its face from the start. . . . Just as the other parties use all the means at their disposal to reach the goals they desire, we should also use *Die Frauenwelt* to penetrate into the broad circles of women who are remote from us.[45]

Despite the paucity of its arguments, the Party executive could claim a certain degree of success. In 1925, the total distribution of Social Democratic women's papers (*Die Frauenwelt* and *Die Genossin*) was 112,000, which was only 12,000 less than that of *Die Gleichheit* in the year of its widest circulation (1914). In 1925, however, there were about 22,000 less women in the Party than in 1914. The Party executive's new press formula did not, therefore, have the effect of 'widening the circle of sympathizers'. It was simply that more Party members now read the women's press. This contradiction, however, caused little concern, for the circulation figures were impressive and the Party executive was certain of the backing of the majority. The critics could hence be described as 'bawlers', and the fronts reversed in a curious manner, with the revolutionaries being accused of conservatism and the conformists, in contrast, being praised for their progressiveness. Nobody seems to have protested at this tactic. Amongst the women, who already constituted a minority within the Party, the critics of the Party executive were hopelessly outvoted once more. Marie Juchacz's speech therefore gave the impression that sufficient concessions had now been made to the discontented, and that in future the Party executive would not 'give in' any more.

Needless to say, the demand for the revival of *Die Gleichheit* must have seemed ridiculous in financial terms, if it meant setting up a third women's magazine alongside *Die Frauenwelt* and *Die Genossin*. But this was not what was being suggested. Formerly, too, all published needs had after all been fulfilled by *Die Gleichheit* and its supplements for women and children, and by the women's supplements in the Party papers. To say that the women's desire for a new paper was superfluous because they held enough power in the large local groups to gain influence over their Party paper, was, given the circumstances, a red herring. No congress went by without complaints about the lack of women's influence.

The opportunity to become more actively involved in the Party press was not open to the women at all, for such involvement was sabotaged by the men's resistance. This is proved by the fact that in 1929 there were only one or two women among the 400 to 500 editors of Party newspapers.[46] Marie Juchacz replied to the critics by saying that criticism of the new women's papers need not be taken seriously, as people had always found a lot of fault with *Die Gleichheit* as well. But there was a crucial difference between the criticism of *Die Gleichheit* and that of *Die Frauenwelt*. *Die Gleichheit* had had to defend its high theoretical level against all the wishes of readers and Party members that it should be popularized, and instead of a 'popular form' for the paper Clara Zetkin had demanded greater popular involvement. As far as criticism of the new magazines was concerned, however, the Party executive was on the defensive against the desire for a higher theoretical level and for an 'educational organ', and was upholding its own formula for the press, which took into account the alleged need to 'popularize' socialism. The fronts were thus exactly the opposite of those in the *Gleichheit* debate of 1913. The critical members were demanding theory, while the executive propagated the idea of 'skilled influence on the masses.'

In view of the criticism, it is incomprehensible how the Party executive could seriously believe that 'all needs were taken care of'. The wishes expressed by some members proved that this was by no means the case. The needs were not measured by the voices of the small number of critical women, but by the Party executive's own judgment, which was assured of majority support. The Party would not permit its ideas on the requirements of women's agitation to be questioned, especially since it always knew how to obtain democratic legitimation for them. In the process it was forgotten that the Party executive's policy did not bring women's emancipation a single step nearer.

e/The Discrimination Against Women

The oppositional attitude of sections of the Social Democratic women's movement during the war continued to find expression after 1918. The women's opposition can be explained by their natural pacifism, their exploitation in the war economy, the contradiction between the Party's claim to support women's emancipation and its policy in practice, and the educational work carried out by *Die Gleichheit*. After the war, their feeling of being second-class citizens was further reinforced by their increasing exclusion from the production process, the instrument for which had been provided by Social Democracy in the form of the Demobilization Decrees. Admittedly, there were isolated instances of women trying to justify such measures. At the Görlitz Party Conference in 1921, for example, Mrs Wachenheim said:

> In certain respects the Demobilization Decrees are quite justified, especially in cases where women who enjoy economic security through their husband's work are thereby removed from employment.[47]

But on the whole, the Party was criticised for its involvement in the dismissal of women workers, especially when it emerged that the desired effect of evacuating jobs for returned servicemen was not taking place. In Görlitz in 1921, the workers' involvement in the dismissal of women was pointed out:

It is not only the Government agencies that have made things extremely difficult for the women, for many factory councils have likewise become downright reactionary in this sphere. In many cases women have been dismissed from jobs in the local bodies without anybody being appointed to replace them; rather, their jobs have been divided among the people already there.[48]

Cases were also quoted of women who had been dismissed from public service for having illegitimate children.[49]

Gradually the women became aware of the scale of their defeat:

> Women were brought in in the time of need, when there was a shortage of labour, but now there is a desire to push them aside once more. And this is happening without any real signs of the strong protest which this should have aroused in the ranks of Social Democracy. We are merely the advance guard for the huge army of women who are fighting for equal economic status, economic freedom and intellectual liberty. When . . . the constitution is broken without anything being done about it, when the number of married women in public service is curtailed, when women civil servants who have dutifully worked for 30 years are simply put out on the street, without Social Democracy sharply protesting at what is happening, then that is a sign that in many respects women's equality only exists on paper.[50]

Technically speaking it was true that any special treatment for female civil servants constituted a breach of the constitution, for Article 109 stated that men and women were to have 'fundamentally the same civil rights and obligations' and article 128 ordered the removal of 'all exceptional regulations against women public servants'.[51] It was also true that the Social Democrats had done nothing to oppose this 'breach of the constitution', if the Demobilization Decrees are to be described in this manner, but had actually been a party to it. On the one hand, however, the Constitution was not passed until after the Demobilization Decrees, so that no actual breach of the constitution existed until the validity of the Decrees was extended to 1923 or 1924. On the other hand, the Decrees were an emergency measure, even if the women thought them unsuited to the purpose. Instead of directing themselves against the capitalist relations of production which were responsible for the struggle over jobs and the discrimination against women, the women demanded that the constitution should be respected, even though its impotence was demonstrated precisely by its inability to regulate the economy. It was true that this constitution had been drawn up by the majority bloc of resolutely democratic parties in the Weimar National Assembly, but the social relations for which it was meant to provide the framework remained determined by capitalism. The infringement of the constitution was merely symptomatic of the fact that the legal structure was out of line with the economic relations, or that the necessary things were not happening in the economy to ensure the effectiveness of the constitutional norms. As in the case of other social achievements of the Revolution, such as the eight-hour day and worker's co-determination in economic councils, crucial aspects of women's constitutional equality were liquidated as a result of the crisis. All declarations of the old idea of emancipation, as formulated by Engels, Zetkin and Bebel, remained powerless in face of the economic facts. The formal declaration of equal status and equal rights for all citizens in the constitution was not worth a thing to working women once they lost their jobs as the result of a crisis in the capitalist mode of production. The fact that the constitution was not able to decree away the social inequality between workers and the owners of the means of production left the women workers as dependent as ever on the fluctuations of the business cycle. The economy was not in a position to make a reality of the most important principle of the socialist movement for emancipation, namely women's right to work. The Party was now inevitably passive on the question of transforming the economy, and the women's protests were to no avail. They demanded that:

> The liberation of women . . . must be carried out by the Party and not evaded by every possible means.[52]
>
> (Or:) The Party Conference calls on the Party caucus in the Assemblies of the Reich and the *Länder* to work with the greatest possible emphasis towards the universal realization, without exception, of constitutional equal status for both sexes, and in particular to work for the removal of exceptional regulations against female white collar workers and civil servants (See Article 14 of the Imperial Decree for the Reduction of Personnel).[53]
>
> (Or:) The Regional Party Conference demands that the Party give energetic attention in theory and practice to the aim of realizing its old programmatic principle of 'women's equal right to work.[54]

The ineffectiveness of such appeals is best illustrated by the fact that even in 1930 the Brüning Government's programme of economies envisaged the dismissal of married women from the public service.[55]

A greater theoretical understanding of the real causes of female unemployment was revealed in the resolution on female labour adopted by the Leipzig Conference in 1931. It said:

> The fight to wipe out unemployment has been used by the employers and the forces of reaction to shift the basis of our struggle and to distract from the real causes of unemployment and from effective means of combating them. The SPD declares its most emphatic opposition to the campaign against working women— irrespective of whether they are single or married. . . . We object most sharply to the attempts to stage a struggle between workers in this way. Our demand is not 'struggle against jobs for women' but 'struggle against the capitalist system', which is alone to blame for the increasing unemployment.[56]

The only thing was, that this recognition came too late. No matter how much was said about 'most emphatic opposition', capitalism continued to emerge the winner in all the important political conflicts. After their defeat in the 1920 election, the Social Democrats never again managed to obtain decisive influence over the course of German politics.

Apart from the debate on the press, the decline in the number of women members in the period of inflation, the small percentage of women's votes cast for Social Democracy throughout the period of the Weimar Republic, and the protests against the Party's passive acceptance of women's exclusion from the production process, the women's dissatisfaction was also made manifest in their criticism of the fact that the number of women office-holders in the Party did not correspond to the strength of the female membership. As early as 1920, Anna Blos wrote in *Die Gleichheit*:

> A bourgeois woman recently pointed out that if all went well, there was only one woman high enough on Social Democratic election lists to have good prospects. This was, so to speak, a concession made to the Party's old demand. Many a competent woman has had to stand down to make way for a man. There is not a single electorate where women were put up in proportion to the number of women voters. Frequently the distribution of women was a question of power politics, and the women are the weaker ones.[57]

Proposals made at the Weimar Party Conference in 1919

and at the Kiel Conference in 1927 for the formation of a special women's council or a national women's committee also remained unanswered by the Party executive, or it was recommended that they be rejected.[58]

The men's unwillingness to entrust women with Party work was condemned in a resolution adopted by the Görlitz Party Conference of 1921, which obliged the comrades 'to involve women more than previously in all kinds of work, in public positions, bodies and functions'.[59] As late as 1927, the same resolution was proposed at the Kiel Women's Conference, and was passed on to the Party executive. In Berlin (1924) it was complained: 'Male comrades today still treat us with a sort of irrelevant benevolence, and we ought to change this into due confidence in our achievements.'[60] Another resolution demanded that there should be an assessment of favourable experiences of co-operation between men and women in the Party.[61] The Party executive, admittedly, was not short of an answer on this point either. It was able to shelter behind the opportunities formally left open by the Party constitution, pointing out that women had not taken advantage of the rights they had been given. Where there was justice in the women's demands, they were asked to present them 'in the appropriate manner'.[62] If only they made a more energetic and skilful appearance, they would get what they wanted all right. Such bits of advice were not of much help to the women, however, for they knew from experience that wherever they got really involved, the men united against them, while the Party executive claimed it was powerless to help.

The only thing in which women were successful was in reducing the minimum qualifying number of female members required for a representative on the Party executive. A resolution in this direction was proposed for the first time at the Weimar Party Conference in 1919, and was renewed and adopted in Berlin in 1924 and Heidelberg in 1925.[63] The women demanded and won an alteration in Paragraphs 23 and 17 respectively of the constitution with the result that first 10,000, then 7,500 was laid down as the number of female members which entitled them to send a woman into the Party executive.[64]

On the question of appointing women's secretaries to the regional executives, all efforts came up against the wall of the Party executive's opposition. The women were either reminded of the Party's financial distress, which made it impossible to appoint women's secretaries, or it was claimed that the tasks of the women's

E

movement could be looked after perfectly well by the existing women's secretaries, and that the traditional division of labour by which the women dealt with women's matters had its disadvantages anyway.[65] The way in which the women themselves assessed this division of labour can be seen from a statement made at the Magdeburg Party Conference in 1929:

> We women, who make up a very considerable percentage of the Party, are left the task of recruiting and training the women, and the men are pleased if we don't make any demands on their time at all. At meetings they debate for hours about the most trivial matters. But if we want to discuss things that concern women then time suddenly runs out and the comrades have to go home.[66]

The limitations of men and women to their 'own' affairs certainly had its disadvantages and was hardly an aid to mutual understanding, but at least as far as the women were concerned, it was the only way of getting anything effective done in the Party at all. The mere declaration of solidarity between the sexes in the Party could not alter this fact. In the last analysis, the men were intent on keeping women out of influential positions. This was shown each time the women tried to obtain office. But the appeal for women to show a 'higher' understanding was not without its effect. The resolutions concerning the question of secretaries were all voluntarily withdrawn.[67] The question had still not been settled in 1929, as is shown by Marie Juchacz's report to the Magdeburg Party Conference. On this occasion she even gave her personal backing to the request that secretaries be appointed and added her own voice to the women's complaints that they were held in low esteem by the male party members. Her assessment of the traditional politeness with which the men greeted the women speaks for the fact that her views had developed further:

> The forms of chivalry and deference, which are actually borrowed from feudalism, inevitably turn into brutality and a sort of sexist contempt when the women become independent and express their own political opinions.[68]

Another woman speaker quoted instances of the way in which the men sabotaged the women's attempts to come of age politically. The forms of discrimination which men practised against women in the Party were clearly recognized:

Women have done much to enrich public life and have often been pioneers in the realm of ideas or the arts. But to many such women it is a source of great suffering that while such progress and development are ideologically recognized throughout the world, hostility to the idea of women making a positive contribution is still so strong that in individual cases women are nevertheless prevented from being effective in the long run. What happens in individual cases is that the woman's feeling of inferiority is reinforced regardless of the splendour of her achievements. The way to encourage women is to help them to overcome such feelings of inferiority. The way to discourage them, however, is to reinforce such feelings, and an instinctive inclination towards this is usually there.[69]

It was stated that although women in Germany 'had equal rights, they remained economically and politically unfree', and that the 'transformation of the capitalist private economy into a social community' required 'the cooperation of men as much as of women'. But instead of being able to concentrate all its forces on this goal, the women's movement had to spend a part of them on the struggle against proletarian anti-feminism within the Party. In the Party, as in society, women's equality failed to eventuate despite the fact that it was officially supported by the Party programme and the constitution. The discrimination that women encountered within the Party faithfully reflected their experience in the economy. The good intentions that were undoubtedly present among individual men as regards the realization of the egalitarian principle, at least within the working-class movement, proved too weak when confronted with the pressure of competition, which led them to fear for their prestige, the Party offices and their authority. The effect of this was felt not only in relatively subordinate Party offices, but even in the Party's choice of candidates for Councils, regional parliaments and the Reichstag. The discrimination against women in the choice of candidates provoked the SPD's National Women's Conference in 1924 to adopt the following resolution:

The agitation committee of the women's groups in Württemburg notes with indignation the way in which women have been so little considered in the choice of candidates. As a result, the number of female representatives in the Reichstag has dwindled to eleven. On the national list, Comrade Juchacz was placed only fifth. We hold the view that our Party, which boasts of being the first and only advocate of equal rights for women, ought to involve women in its work to a much greater extent. Their present representation bears no relation to the number of women voters.[70]

We can conclude from this resolution that the decline in the number of female Members of Parliament was not due to the fact that women candidates were not elected, but that the Party had not allowed as many women to stand in the first place.

Table 4 shows a clear decline in the number of female SPD representatives. In the case of borough councillors and city councillors, this decline is particularly marked in 1925 as compared with the relative maximum of 1924, but it also went below the level of 1919/20. Marie Juchacz attributed this to the fact that 'the women have not presented their justified demands in the appropriate manner'.[71] But this explanation once more blames the women for a situation which was caused by the men of the Party in the first instance. The SPD reached its highest percentage of female Members of Parliament in 1928. At that time there were 20 women (13.1 per cent of the Social Democratic MPs) in the caucus. In 1924, the percentage of women in the Social Democratic caucus was 12.2 per cent; in the remaining years, it never rose above 11.5 per cent. The fact that the women made up 15.8 per cent of the Party membership in 1924, 21.2 per cent in 1928 and even 23 per cent in 1932,[72] shows the discrimination unmistakably. The women's

Table 4

Survey of female SPD Members of Parliament.[73]

Body	1919-20[a]	1920-21[b]	1924[c]	1925[d]	1927[e]	1929[f]	1930[g]
Municipalities	413	410	484	197	452	?	?
Town councils	1	1	4	—	—	?	?
City councillors	386	466	506	270	295	?	?
Local boards and mayors	24	5	10	1	—	?	?
District Assemblies	1	8	10	—	?	?	?
Provincial Assemblies (and the Prussian Assembly)	2	6	13	61	63	53	52

| | NA | 1stR | 2ndR | 3rdR | 4thR | 5thR | 6thR | 7thR |
	1919	1920	1924	1924	1928	1930	1932	1932
National Assembly (NA) or Reichstag[h]	19	13	11	16	20	16	15	14

lack of political education and intellectual backwardness alone cannot account for this, for in the given circumstances it was already a sign of advanced political consciousness for a woman to be a member of the Social Democratic Party at all. The small number of female representatives was the result of the way in which Social Democratic MPs were recruited. Most of them came from the Party or the trade-union bureaucracy, in which the women only had weak representation.

The number of women elected to the lower committees of local government show that the Party failed, at least in the first five years, in its attempts to open up a specifically feminine field of activity for women in social work. But even in 1927, the Social Democratic women provided only 10.5 per cent of the MPs in the regional assemblies, 4 per cent in the provincial assemblies, 4.3 per cent of city councillors and 1.5 per cent of borough councillors.[74]

f/Women's Social Work

After the decline from 1920 to 1923, the number of female members began to increase again, and hence there was also a growth in the number of women who wanted to share in the work and responsibilities of the Party. We have shown in our discussion of the debate on the press, the question of secretaries, and the choice of candidates, how the Party executive sought to evade their demands. Under pressure from the women, the executive inevitably saw the idea of opening up a specifically feminine area of work as a pat solution to the difficulties posed by the possibility of women becoming radicalized. It is in this context that a statement at the Görlitz Party Conference must be interpreted: 'The pressure from women comrades for a positive share in our work is being met by the Central Committee for Workers' Welfare.'[75] This committee's task was to organize working class participation in welfare work, to recruit new forces and to arrange cooperation with similar organizations. 'On this question too, therefore, the workers' guiding thought is 'Not to be merely the object, but also the subject of welfare work.'[76]

However plausible this guiding principle may seem, it is equally absurd when measured by the old socialist demands. Viewed in this light it looks as if, after having failed to break the power of capitalism, the workers wanted at least to establish the 'right' to

relieve by themselves the distress caused by capitalism and which
the Government's own welfare agencies could not cope with. As
long as Workers' Welfare was seen as a way for workers who were
not adequately looked after by the state to help themselves, then
that was in line with its real function. But the new motto about
the 'subjects of welfare' was meant to signify something more as
well: the democratization of public relief, the 'injection of the
workers' own social attitude' into Welfare.[77] How little this concept
corresponded to the reality can be measured by a report, given at
the Görlitz Party Conference in 1921, on the first meagre results.
It stated:

> With the cooperation of the Ministry of the Interior, the various
> trade unions, and women's schools of social work, about 120
> women (chosen on a pro rata basis) have been given a training
> course in social work. The recently declared intention of the
> national and regional governments to provide bursaries for women
> with primary school education to take the regular courses at the
> women's schools for social work is also due, among other things,
> to the efforts of the central Committee for Workers' Welfare.[78]

The disproportion between these data and the number of
female Members of Parliament on the one hand, and the claim
about the 'injection of the workers' own social attitude' on the other,
could be given no clearer expression than this. Needless to say,
welfare work certainly had its place, precisely in the sense that it
supplemented state relief and provided the individual worker who
had got into difficulty with assistance from a workers' organization
and thus a concrete expression of solidarity. The myth of the
'subjects of welfare work' however, could only serve to hide the
fact that self-determination in welfare was the corollary of deter-
mination by others in the economy and society. Social work was
merely a way of providing an extremely limited training in welfare
practices, and the exercise of these practices with inadequate means,
and served to channel women's activity into the harmless sphere
of 'useful' work. It was not, however, a way of educating people
politically towards socialism and towards effective self-help. The
Party executive appears to have missed this point, however. Instead,
it proclaimed:

> The area of local government offers a vast field of activity to the
> proletarian woman. There is still a great deal of ground here for
> women to become publicly effective, for in the first rank of the

many problems that may be solved in this sphere in the future are the problems of socialization.[79] (And:) Many people are today unable to find a field of activity in the Party which corresponds to their individuality and in which they can prove their worth. Workers' Welfare is the organization which now provides such a field. We can observe how women in particular are devoting themselves to this movement with all their heart and soul and with a great willingness to sacrifice. The organization gives our women comrades the inner satisfaction of being able to work within the Party for the benefit of the broad general public.[80]

It would be hard to find a better description of the essence of Workers' Welfare: it was a safe outlet for the excess energy which misguided women had originally wanted to transform into political action, but which was now guided into the genuinely feminine, motherly social sphere. Now that 'inner satisfaction' had replaced political action, everyone could be satisfied: the women, because they were 'systematically occupied and receiving additional training'[81]—and the Party executive, because it had transformed threatening forces into useful ones. The ideology of social work was thus a combination of many factors: the powerlessness of the working-class movement in face of the increasingly reactionary policy of its political opponents, the women's desire for involvement in the Party and the Party executive's need to defend itself against the uncomfortable rebelliousness and criticism of the women with regard to discrimination against them.

If anyone objected to the programme on the grounds that far too little money was available for the really large tasks of social welfare, the frugal housewives took the floor and extolled the virtues of modesty, which can get things organized even with meagre resources:

> There is advantage to be gained, for example, even from the simple fact of our male and female comrades getting the local councils to allow people to visit the institutions to which children are sent by the state, without having to make an appointment first. If the women acquire a really decisive influence in this sphere, then that could pave the way for achieving a great deal more still.[82]

All these factors were ingeniously woven into an address given by Frau Dr Schöfer on the subject of 'Women's Social Work in the Local Community' at the SPD's National Women's Conference in Görlitz in 1921.

She began by asking whether there really were any such things as women's own social tasks in the local community, and seemed to deny that there were by pointing to the Party's advocacy of 'universal human rights' rather than special demands for women. It was her belief, however, that one should not narrow-mindedly reject the view, which was also taken by many Social Democrats, that women ought to be excluded from general questions concerning the community and be allocated to the area of social work. If it was claimed that this area was ideally suited to women, then she could only endorse that view for,

> Woman is the born guardian and protectress of human life; that is why social work must seem so very appropriate to her. By allocating to women the task of guarding over human life we simultaneously provide a positive answer to the question whether women have a task in politics at all.[83]

The sequence of thought was skilful: starting from the question whether there were any special tasks for women, she then touched on the rejection of such a standpoint by the Party's doctrine. This however, was immediately watered down by the opposite view 'of many Social Democrats'. When the validity of the old theory of women's emancipation had thus been thrown into question, the anti-feminist thesis that the woman's place was in the home was picked up, with slight modifications, 'by allocating to women the task of guarding over human life'. No reason was given for this. The question as to why these tasks were 'so ideally suited' to the woman was not answered, except by the tautology that social work is so appropriate for women because they are the guardians of human life. This proposition, which was only seemingly thrown into question, then appeared as the compelling outcome of a sequence of thought, while it was in fact merely the unproven presupposition. However, since the majority of the women, as of the men, shared this assumption, Frau Schöfer needed to have no fear that her illogical train of thought would be exposed. So she could say:

> If struggle is more appropriate to the male manner, so the woman knows better how to guard and preserve human life. If the male knows more about the goods economy and the production of goods, so the woman is better suited to immerse herself in human destinies.[84]

Thus far, everything was a faithful repetition of the familiar phrases about the natural division of labour between the sexes; the only variation consisted in the fact that the female sphere of activity had been widened to include welfare, but this had already been the domain of charitable ladies in the past. The only differences between 'Workers' Welfare' and such charity was that the former was the workers' own relief organization and did not proceed out of the philanthropic inclinations of the upper class of society.

Frau Schöfer did not stop at showing women the opportunities for sharing in the Party's work that were inherent in 'Workers' Welfare'. Just like the Party executive, which had talked about the problems of socialization being solved at the level of the local councils,[85] she was looking for an ideological transfiguration of social work. She found it in the motto of a 'human economy' entrusted to women.

> Human economy is the deployment of people as a value-factor in the economy. . . . Apart from their function as the propagators of human life, women have the job of giving individual human life the most productive and happy form that is possible.[86]
>
> They [the women comrades—WT] must untiringly emphasize this principle . . . They must show the representatives of the bourgeoisie, and their own comrades, the real meaning of thrift. They must make it clear to them that the thrift which forces human lives to make do with less than the necessary means of existence, is misplaced, and that a thrifty approach to human life constitutes greater thrift than a thrifty approach to material economic goods.[87]
>
> It is women's task to get the idea of the economy of human lives accepted in politics.[88]

According to Frau Schöfer, therefore, women were now to achieve what the Social Democratic Party had failed to do until then: create a situation in which the person did not exist for the process of production, but the process of production for the person. That was the idea behind the abstruse formula of the 'human economy' in which the real humanism of the Socialists had found refuge. It was not simply a matter of the old idea being given a new name, however, for the thing itself was changed along with the concept. In conformance with Taylorism and psychotechnology, which had discovered that it paid off economically to give heed to the 'human factor in business', the 'person as value' was now to be introduced into politics and the economy. Capitalism was to be humanized by being shown that it would do best, in terms of its own principle of the economic use of all productive forces, to 'take a thrifty approach to human life'.

Frau Schöfer's concept presented the Social Democratic women who had been sent into welfare work and committees of local government with the magic formula of the 'human economy' which, even if it would not overcome capitalism itself, would still erase blatant forms of exploitation and opposition.

Even though Frau Schöfer's speculations were voiced before the supreme body of the women's movement and in the presence of representatives from the Party executive, nobody spoke out against them in order to point out their incompatibility with socialist conceptions in general and the theory of women's emancipation in particular. When it came to the point the expectations that the Party attached to the deployment of women in social work were not substantially different from Frau Schöfer's 'human economy'. Very little separated the latter from the formulations of Party executive member Wutzky about the 'solution of the problems of socialization in the sphere of the local councils'.

The ideological trimmings which Frau Schöfer put around social work for the benefit of the women did not prevent them from providing some relief to the distress of the working class.

Some idea of the activity of 'Workers' Welfare' is given by the Social Democratic Yearbooks which came out annually from 1926. In 1928, the annual report on 'Workers' Welfare' quotes 208 training courses lasting 1–6 months with 2–4 hours a week, 291 working groups lasting 1–6 months with 2–4 hours a week, 1,152 single lectures and 69 welfare conferences lasting 1–3 days. It reports that in the year in question Workers' Welfare had supported an occupational training school, two children's homes, one residential hostel, one convalescent home and innumerable sewing workshops.[89]

In 1930 there were 2,000 local committees of 'Workers' Welfare', more than half of which were combined with advisory centres; 500 local committees ran sewing workshops possessing a total of 2,000 sewing machines. Areas of work named by the report were: care for unemployed girls, combined with training in handicraft and housework, the feeding of children and the unemployed, care of pregnant women and domestic help given by 2,000 volunteers, the lending out of baby equipment, and cooperation in public welfare work. Helpers were attracted through 64 working groups, 124 week-end courses, 28 longer courses, 1,200 single lectures and 15,000 meetings. The national leadership courses held by the Central Committee of Workers' Welfare were continued. Apart from this, there was a study fund, and a publishing house which published the periodical *Arbeiterwohlfahrt (Workers' Welfare)*, a number of textbooks and outlines for lectures.[90]

Increasing unemployment gave added importance to 'Workers' Welfare'. Its achievements, however, must not obscure the fact that by restricting women to social work it perpetuated discrimination with other means. Despite the achievement of legal equality, women were condemned as before to the 'politique du foyer', and all that had happened was that the 'foyer' was made a little larger. Women had been on the point of breaking out of existing society politically, but they were reintegrated once more by being allocated a special function in social administration, and the damage to men was kept down to a minimum.[91]

8/Economic and Organizational Stabilization

When discussing the fluctuations in membership within the SPD we pointed out that the number of women members reached its lowest ebb in the very year (1923) that inflation was at its peak. The year 1923 was also marked by the highest level of unemployment of any of the first five post-war years, and this affected women more severely than men in relation to their share of the employed work force. The women's share in the Party was 10.3 per cent in 1923. For the whole period from 1910 to 1931, this was the lowest it went, in both absolute and relative terms.

The 'blossoming' of the German economy as from 1924, by which was meant the fact that despite unemployment production was being stepped up, was set in motion by foreign capital and encouraged by rationalization.

> Within the work force semi-skilled and unskilled labour, including female labour, began to take strong precedence over skilled labour. There was a massive upswing in the number of white collar workers. But among these, it was the less qualified people—in the case of the technical workers, the foreman as opposed to the old-style master craftsmen, in the case of clerical workers, the people who did mechanical machine work, particularly women typists and adding machine operators—who gained the upper hand.[1]

Female labour in agriculture and forestry had been on the decline ever since 1907, and this trend continued till 1933. The number of women employed in industry and manual labour increased by 893,413 from 1907 to 1925, but fell by 261,441 from 1925 to 1933. This does not take into account the level of female labour during the war. It can be assumed, however, that the increase between 1907 and 1925 was not distributed evenly over all these years, that it was especially large during the war and very small, in contrast, in the post-war years. The number of women employed in trade and transport increased by 79,005 from 1907 to 1925, but by 132,977 from 1925 to 1933, bringing the percentage of women engaged in this branch of the economy up to 21.57 per cent.

The total share of female labour barely changed from 1907 (33.8 per cent) to 1933 (35.6 per cent). The female population increased by 15.5 per cent between 1907 and 1925, which contrasts with an increase of 30.5 per cent in the number of able-bodied women between the ages of 16 and 65 and a rise of 35 per cent in the number of women employed. The increase in the number of women in employment thus corresponds almost exactly to the growth in female population. A look at the distribution of the flow of new women into production over the various branches of the economy reveals that the increase in the number of clerical workers, which was already under way in 1907, is particularly prominent.

Within this group, the number of technical workers rose by 120.5 per cent from 1907 to 1925, the number of women foremen and supervisors declined by 29.9 per cent and there was an increase of 497.1 per cent in the number of female shop and office workers. The first two groups together rose by 91.3 per cent from 1925 to 1933, while the last group fell by 7 per cent. The greatest increase was recorded by the group of women employed in business and transport.

In the remaining female occupations there was little change between 1925 and 1933.[2]

A survey of members carried out by Susanne Suhr on behalf of the Central Association of White Collar Workers provides a good general picture of the situation of female white collar workers between 1925 and 1930.[3] The author attributes the increase in the number of women white-collar workers to the women surplus created by the war, rationalization and the impoverishment of the middle class. Before 1925, there had been a tendency for women workers to move from domestic work to industry, but after this time there was an influx of domestic and textile workers into white-collar jobs, which became an increasingly typical form of female labour. Out of approximately 1.4 million female white collar workers in 1930, only 10–11 per cent were paid the same as men, 9 per cent had less than 10 per cent diminution in the going rate for the job, 65 per cent suffered a loss of 10 per cent, and 16 per

cent lost more than 10 per cent. Apart from this, 14 per cent of all
female white-collar workers were paid below the award rates, i.e.
even less. Fierce competition therefore developed with male white-
collar workers. The campaign against the so-called 'double earners',
working wives of working men, was unfair in the case of women
white collar workers, however, for 92 per cent of them were single
and only 8 per cent married. In order to abolish the involuntary
'competition with unfair means', the Central Association demanded
equal pay for men and women. The extent to which female white-
collar workers were affected by general unemployment in these
years can be seen by the fact that the number of female shop and
office workers registered as looking for work at the employment
offices in July of each year, the month of least demand for workers,
was 16,858 in 1925, 60,594 in 1926, 48,396 in 1927, 45,591 in
1928 and 61,680 in 1929.

The results of the 1925 census of population and employment,
from which most of the information given by Preller and Susanne
Suhr derives, also attracted the attention of the Social Democratic
women's movement. Anna Siemsen published an article on the
subject in the *Sozialistische Monatshefte* in 1928, in which she
stressed that 48 per cent of female labour consisted of helping
out in family enterprises. This type of work, however, was marked
by an especial lack of independence. Concerning women's motives
in getting married, she wrote:

> Women are faced with fierce competition economically, suffer from
> men's defensive attitude and enjoy few prospects of a career, so
> they naturally turn to marriage as a way out. What is unhealthy
> is not that women should want to get married, but that in marriage
> they should seek the security and improvement of their situation
> which they do not find in their jobs.[4]

Marie Juchacz discussed the 1925 census of population and
employment in a detailed report on 'Women in the Economy' at
the Magdeburg Party Conference in 1929. To summarize what
she had to say she quoted the conclusion of the Annual Report of
the German Federation of Trade Unions

> that female labour will not decline in the future, not even in times
> when the business cycle is more favourable to the men, for there
> is a general need for it in economic life and the desire for
> personal freedom, which is inseparable from economic inde-
> pendence, is already far too strongly developed.

In explicit reference to the 'old literature' ('Bebel, *Die Gleich-heit*, Lily Braun') she said:

> Any assessment of the scope of women's involvement in political
> life, and the degree of its intensity, must proceed from the women's
> economic situation and their involvement in economic life.[5]

The vast programme of dismissals in the post-war years was
followed by an increase in female employment during the period of
economic upswing in which white-collar jobs had the greatest share.
But because this development was accompanied by a steady rise
in the level of unemployment, a similar tension arose between
men and women to that which existed under the regime of the
Demobilization Decrees up till 1923. In the earlier period, the
state had encouraged the dismissal of women, but now the rationalization of the German economy after 1924 promoted their employment. Apart from this, the women were pressing for jobs for the
very reason that the men were unemployed. At the same time as
male unemployment grew, there was an increase in the labour pool
of married women.[6]

Just as in the period before 1923, the unemployed saw the
dismissal of women as a suitable means of fighting unemployment.
This was shown by corresponding resolutions at the Social Democratic Party Conference in 1929 and 1931, which were directed
against attempts 'to stage a struggle of workers amongst each
other in this manner'.[7] The Leipzig resolution was evidence of the
fact that the Social Democrats now recognized that the struggle
against female labour was a manoeuvre designed to distract the
working class from the real causes of unemployment inherent in
capitalism itself. This insight determined the outcome of the discussion on the so-called 'double earners'. Under the rule of the
Demobilization Decrees women had been forced out of production.
The women's movement had suffered a severe setback as a result.
The increase in female labour brought a gradual improvement in the
Party membership. Marie Juchacz described this development as a
'general organizational healing process.'[8]

As a result of the departure of many men from the Party, but
also of an increase in the number of women itself, the women's
share in the membership rose from 10.3 per cent (1923) to 21.2
per cent (1928). The percentage of female members was maintained
in the period of inflation despite increased unemployment, and rose
to 23 per cent in 1931.[9]

The connexion between women's employment and Party membership, which was stressed as early as the Görlitz Party Conference in 1921 and which was also in line with the socialist theory of women's emancipation, was made clear once again by this 'healing process'. It was not just the number of female Party members that increased: Marie Juchacz was able to report in Leipzig (1931):

> We are also seeing an increase in women's attendance at meetings and a growing interest by women in day-to-day political matters. Women are of course today so strongly affected by day-to-day political matters that such interest must grow automatically. The question of wage reductions and the fight against fascism are also of the greatest importance to women for they feel their political freedom threatened.[10]

Table 5

Survey of changes in membership in the SPD and the trade unions between 1918 and 1931.[11]

Year	Total Party Membership[a]	Women[a]	Per cent Women[a]	Total Trade Union Membership[b]	Women[b]	Per cent Women[b]
1918	249,411	66,000	26.8	1,664,991[c]	442,957[c]	26.6[c]
1919	1,012,299	207,000	20.5	5,479,078[c]	1,192,767[c]	21.8[c]
1920	1,180,208	207,000	17.5	6,179,341	1,710,761	27.7
1921	1,221,059	192,485	14.1	6,049,361	1,518,341	26.1
1922	1,174,105	?	?	?	?	?
1923	1,261,072	130,000	10.3	5,537,003	1,526,155	27.6
1924	940,078	148,125	15.8	3,643,023	921,140	25.3
1925	844,495	153,693	18.2	3,404,866	751,585	22.1
1926	823,529	165,492	20.1	3,317,816	659,499	19.9
1927	867,671	181,541	20.8	3,735,181	680,508	18.2
1928	937,381	198,771	21.2	4,127,281	739,645	17.9
1929	949,306	201,000	21.2	4,229,663	718,604	17.0
1930	1,037,384	228,278	22.0	4,047,284	669,285	16.5
1931	1,008,953	230,331	23.0	3,564,060	570,836	16.0

A comparison between membership changes in the Party and in the free trade unions (see Table 5) reveals that both organizations had their maximum number of female members in 1920. A decline then followed in the trade unions, which lasted until 1926, when there was a slight increase until 1928, followed again by a substantial decline until 1931. From 1923 to 1924 the percentage of women in the free trade unions fell by 37 per cent. In 1924, women made up only 18.8 per cent of the membership as compared with 21.8 per cent in 1919.[12] In the Party, the number of female members declined heavily from 1920 to 1923, rose steadily from 1924 to 1931 and exceeded the 1920 peak by 11,278 in 1930 and 23,331 in 1931. The trade unions never regained the 1920 level of female members. Even in 1931 they still had 1,139,925 less women than in 1920.

The political wing of the women's movement was thus strengthened in relation to the trade-union wing. After 1924, the Social Democratic women increased their efforts in order to win for the Party the women who were just entering the production process. The recruitment and education of female members were both intensified and increased substantially. In 1926, the Party held 25 women's conferences in 19 regions.

In 1927, a national women's conference was held in Kiel in conjunction with the Party Conference. The principal topic was the housing question, but there was also discussion of the problems involved in recruiting new members for the Party, the work of recruitment and education, the law to combat sexual disease, agitation against the abortion paragraphs and improvements to the controversial newspapers of the women's movement. The Women's Bureau that year spent its time sending out circulars, winter programmes, guidelines, speakers' outlines, pamphlets and recruitment letters. It published a questionnaire to record experiences in women's agitation and once more held the traditional 'International Women's Conference'.[13]

In the following year the women's movement concentrated its efforts on preparing for the Reichstag elections. The Women's Bureau took part in the election campaign with pamphlets, films, posters, and special courses. The 1928 *Social Democratic Yearbook* says of the women's movement:

Today there is no region that cannot report regional and sub-regional conferences and courses, weekend seminars and regular women's evenings. In the country as a whole the current year has seen 22 regional conferences, 167 sub-regional conferences, and 159 courses of various kinds for women.

Under the theme of 'Social Democratic Community Politics', the leadership course dealt with local autonomy, by-laws and municipal constitutions, economy, local policy, cultural policy, and the councils' social tasks. The women also participated in the regional holiday courses (190 women and 561 men) and the Party's itinerant science courses (389 women and 1891 men). The International Women's Conference in Brussels in August 1928 discussed the socialist demands of the working-class movement's political wing and the trend towards the mobilization of women in times of war.[14]

Table 6

Survey of women's education in the SPD[15]

1926	District Conferences for Women	25[a]
1928	District Conferences for Women	22[b]
	Sub-District Conferences	167[b]
	Various Types of Courses for Women	159[b]
1930	District Courses	20[c]
	Sub-District Courses	63[c]
	Local Courses	162[c]
1931	District, Sub-District and Local Courses	351[d]
	District and Sub-District Conferences	71[d]

The Social Democratic women's movement also took part in the fight against the National Socialists. A special working group was set up, which comprised female representatives from the General German Federation of Trade Unions, the Federation of White Collar Workers, the workers' sports organizations, the Young Socialist Workers and the Party. It was intended to attract working women to the Social Democratic Party. The motto of the International Women's Conference in 1931 was 'Against war and Nazi terrorism, for socialism and peace'. On the day of the conference, over 500 meetings were held throughout the country, at which resolutions were passed condemning the Nazis and Paragraph 218 of the penal code. The agitation was intended to halt the growing influx of women into the Nazi Party. To scare women away from the Nazis, the *Gewerkschaftliche Frauenzeitung* published a collection of earlier statements by leading officials of the National Socialist Workers' Party condemning female labour and quoting analogies from the animal world to support the view that the women's place was in the home.[16]

In 1931, *Die Genossin,* the organ for the women officials of the Social Democratic Party, reached a circulation of 40,000 copies.[17]

9/The Open Door Movement

Women socialists from individual countries had very early (at the International Women's Conference in Zurich in 1893 for example) expressed reservations about the introduction of special protection for women workers, on the grounds that such protective legislation would lead to discrimination against women, for employers preferred workers who were not protected by special laws.[1] Nonetheless, international Social Democracy did advocate far-reaching measures for the protection of women. The exclusion of women from the production process during the crises of the post-war economy, however, gave new impetus to the forces opposed to female protection. At a conference of the World League for Women's Suffrage in Paris in 1926, a resolution was adopted with a slim majority rejecting the idea of any special protection for women workers. The *Gewerkschaftliche Frauenzeitung* attributed this to the presence of numerous women from the East who were still so far removed from any form of emancipation that they saw as their highest goal the achievement of absolute equality with men, as propagated by the Scandinavians and the English.[2]

The International Trade Union Women's Conference, held in 1927, expressed itself in favour of adequate protection for women workers, although the Danish and Swedish delegates abstained.[3] Despite this, an 'International Open Door Council' was set up in Berlin in June 1929. According to a spokeswoman for the organization, its aim was to obtain the same protection for men as had previously been granted only to women. They claimed that the protection of workers should be governed by the nature of the job rather than the sex of the worker, as otherwise restrictions would be imposed on people's personal liberty.[4] The SPD condemned the Open Door Council[5] and the Women's Committee of the Socialist International likewise expressed its opposition to the movement, which above all drew its support from the Scandinavians, on the grounds that it was directed against the interests of working women.[6]

The consequences of the Demobilization Decrees in Germany had already shown that any policy that fought against the symptoms of unemployment, such as dismissals and the shortage of jobs, rather than its causes, would only improve the workers' situation to the extent that the men obtained higher wages and salaries. The corollary of growing male unemployment, however, was an increase in women's demand for jobs, and precisely because women's wages were lower than men's, they were more sought-after as workers. Rising unemployment not only added the unemployed themselves to the industrial reserve army, but also hundreds of thousands of women who found themselves 'diving into the labour market' in order to find a job at the slightest shock to their working-class household budget.[7] As a result of the growing pressure of the industrial reserve army, women's wages showed a tendency to drop in comparison with men's from 1926 to 1932.[8] While women were increasingly being forced to work and their real wages were falling, the Open Door Council now sought to tear down even the final barrier to the exploitation of women by demanding that the regulations for female protection be adapted to those for the protection of workers in general. Admittedly, it claimed that it stood, on the contrary, for the extension of women's protection to all workers. But this demand did not make sense, on the one hand, because some of the regulations for women's protection were not even applicable to men, and on the other, because after 1929 the erosion of social legislation became increasingly obvious. Furthermore, the fighting strength of the trade unions was also weakened in financial terms by the growth of unemployment.[9] Under such circumstances, it was impossible even to consider extending the advantages of women's protection to men even where they were applicable. Social Democracy and the trade unions therefore felt that the demands of the Open Door Council amounted to the abolition of protection for women workers, with the aim of increasing even further the 'advantage' of underpaying of female labour through the lapse of restrictive regulations on female workers. This would only intensify the rivalry between male and female workers, and women's working conditions would be pushed back by decades. The anxiety felt by supporters of the Open Door Movement that women's protection was restraining employers from employing women, was based on a false assumption. They overlooked the fact that restrictions placed on the exploitation of female workers by protective legislation were more than compensated for by the underpayment of women. Clara Zetkin had pointed this out as long ago as 1893. At that time she wrote in *Die Gleichheit*:

> What would happen if the capitalist employers should carry out their threats and reply to the introduction of a mandatory normal working day for women and to the other regulations for their protection by firing all their women workers? In place of the cheap workers they fired, they would have to employ expensive male workers, who might even become dearer in the event . . . The capitalist who, when faced with these facts, would want to do without women industrial workers, and thus without fat profits, has not yet been born and his parents are already dead.[10]

While the Open Door Movement got itself entangled in the contradictions of wanting to abolish protection for women workers for the women's own sake, Social Democracy and the trade unions recognized that it was not in the interests of the working class to intensify the rivalry between male and female workers. The abolition of women's protection would have made no difference to the general unemployment (since it could not increase the number of jobs), and would have drawn the attention of the Party and the trade unions away from the struggle against the ruling system and directed it to a superficial phenomenon. It would have deepened the already present antagonism between men and women and thus further weakened the solidarity of the working-class movement. On top of all this, it would have increased the exploitation of women and made their working conditions worse.

By their opposition to the Open Door Council, and to the campaign against the concept of the 'double earners', by their emphasis on women's equal right to work, even when married, and by interpreting the struggle between male and female labour as the result of the capitalist relations of production[11] the Social Democratic women's movement after 1929 rediscovered its former theory of women's emancipation. As in the case of the reaction after 1917, this revival too must be viewed in the context of the overall situation of the working-class movement. It was true that the SPD was outside the Government in the period of stabilization from 1924 to

1928, but by its opposition and positive suggestions it was capable of exercising a substantial amount of influence over social legislation. Admittedly, its membership in 1929 was about the same as in 1924, but in conjunction with the free trade unions it managed 'to raise the standard of life of the workers from the low level to which it had sunk during the inflation and the first months of stabilization'.[12] We have already mentioned the fact that even in these relatively favourable years of the post-war period unemployment and short-time work reached a substantial scale. The 1928 Reichstag elections, in which the Social Democrats polled 9 million votes, brought them their greatest victory since 1919.[13] They formed a Coalition Government under the Social Democrat Hermann Müller. The plans of the cabinet majority to make substantial cuts in spending on social services led to the resignation of the Social Democrats in March. There followed the Brüning Government, which no longer governed with a Parliamentary majority but on the basis of the emergency Paragraph 48 of the Weimar Constitution. In the 1930 Reichstag elections, the National Socialists polled 6.5 million votes. It was a sign of the end of the Weimar period.[14]

The healing process which had begun in the period of stabilization had brought many new members into the women's movement. The movement had reinforced its work of recruitment and education, and just like the SPD, it was on the upward path in 1928. This seemed to justify the policy that had been followed up till then, but any such belief was shattered by the economic crisis which began in 1929. The increasingly radical tenor of the proceedings at the Magdeburg Party Conference, and even more so at the Leipzig Congress, stood in stark contrast to the earlier attitude. It was undoubtedly due to the fact that the women's movement saw its achievements threatened by the intensified rivalry between men and women on the labour market, the erosion of social services, mass unemployment and the mounting danger of fascism.

A united front SPD–KPD that ruthlessly waged war upon Brüning's dictatorship and capitalism might still have decided the destiny of the German Republic by compelling the new Nazi electorate to decide between Capitalism and Socialism. . . . Since, however, the KPD leaders did not want a revolution, but only wished to follow the easy road of making propaganda against the SPD, and since the Right-wing Socialist leaders mistrusted the power of the proletariat and preferred the 'lesser evil', no such united Socialist fighting front came into existence.[15]

The last official figures put the number of female members at 230,000 in 1931. This exceeded the maximum of 1918–19 by 23,000.[16] This increase in membership had no more political effect, however, than the apparently radical statements on the woman question made at the final Party Conferences.

Conclusion

At the close of the seventy-year period in which we have investigated the theoretical and political manifestations of Social Democracy in the field of women's liberation stands the total annihilation of the socialist workers' movement in Germany. With it perished the most important achievements of the women's movement.

The defeat of the working-class movement and the women's movement is proof of the inseparability of the latter from the emancipation of society as a whole. The fate of both can be traced back to a single cause: the inability to make socialism a reality. The working class could not sit passively and wait for the capitalist economy to collapse or watch without doing anything while the working class sank into increasing poverty, but neither did it have sufficient force to achieve the overthrow of the old society. This dichotomy between its ultimate goal and the real possibilities forced the working-class movement to adopt a policy of reform in the context of the existing order. The political and trade-union organization of the proletariat was intended to relieve immediate distress and also increase the forces for the revolution. It was believed that social reform would enable the workers who were at present oppressed by their living conditions to take an active part in Social Democracy's political struggle. The Social Democratic Party drew up its principles of women's emancipation with this in mind, and at the same time these principles were intended to overcome the attitude of proletarian anti-feminism. They combined the recognition that female labour made the dissolution of the old family relations inevitable with the demand for practical measures to improve the women's living and working conditions. It was Clara Zetkin's conviction that the road to economic independence led through the 'wilderness of exploitation'. On the other hand, the

women would not have any opportunity to take part in the proletarian class struggle until 'the eight-hour day and the right of free
combination and association had been wrested from the capitalist
state'.[1] But while the socialist theorists remained conscious of the
essential link between revolution and reform, the two increasingly
diverged in the actual politics of the working-class movement. The
parliamentary caucus of Social Democracy, which always remained
smaller than that of the bourgeois parties before 1918 despite the
growing number of Social Democratic voters, could only exercise
an indirect influence on social legislation, for which it compensated
with theoretical 'decisiveness'. But in the meantime, the growing
trade-union movement, which was anxious to pursue a policy of
immediately useful reforms, was steadily increasing in importance.
The actions of neither the parliamentary caucus nor the trade
unions, however, pointed beyond the economic foundations of
existing society. On the other hand, the steady increase in
the membership of the working-class movement gave rise to the
hope that it would be possible to seize state power by legal
means.

The position of women within the Party was quite different
in the periods of extensive and intensive capitalist exploitation.

In the era of extensive exploitation, the women's distress was
so great, their working conditions so bad, and their domestic
relations so oppressive, that there was little chance of awakening
their political interest. Only very few women of bourgeois origin,
and even fewer women workers, found intellectual access to
socialism and contact with Social Democracy. Proletarian anti-
feminism predominated among the male workers.

In the following period, when capitalism turned from its
methods of unbridled exploitation to more intensive labour and
greater productivity, there was an improvement in the workers'
situation. Working hours were reduced, and numerous protective
measures were introduced. Workers became capable of recognizing
their own situation, and the working-class movement obtained
significance as a factor in politics. Wherever the Social Democratic
campaign of enlightenment stirred women into action, they were
even more resolute than the men for they bore a two-fold burden:
if they had shaken off their economic dependence from the male
by themselves becoming wage-workers, they were still paid less
than the men and equally felt the pressures of the business cycle.
But even if they had not yet been drawn into industrial production,

their experience of dependence on the male and of his dependence on the laws of the economy enabled them to recognize the contradiction between themselves and existing society. Even the socialists who supported women's liberation and regarded the principle of equal rights for the female sex, as propagated by the Party, as a political goal, were affected by the workings of competition, which used the existence of an industrial reserve army to play off female labour against male labour. Such competition penetrated right into the life of the family, and was made even worse by the time-honoured traditions of a male-dominated society. In its criticism of the existing social system, Social Democratic agitation concentrated on wage and price policies, import duties, children's protection and military affairs, and by this means non-working women were attracted to the Party as well. Such women were now able to see concrete reasons for their vague feeling of discontent in the socio-economic structure and the ruling conditions were stripped of their semblance of necessity and inalterability.

To the extent that the working class no longer saw itself the helpless object of the ruling classes, it also became more attractive to women; the Party's persecution under the anti-Socialist Law reinforced the feeling of men and women in the working-class movement that they belonged together, and this feeling was developed into class consciousness by theory.

By the time the Party returned to legality, women had been found who devoted themselves with extraordinary intellectual vigour to the task of organizing and educating women workers. Once something had been recognized as right, they clung to it stubbornly, and after the turn of the century they reaped the reward of a vast growth in the women's movement. Clara Zetkin, in particular, both developed the socialist theory of women's emancipation to its purest form and gave the most effective direction to the agitation and organization of women.

The leap in the membership of the Party in the years that followed, the effects of Bismarck's social legislation and the rise of real wages seemed to bring the definitive victory of the Party within tangible reach.

The reaction to the new position of the Party, summed up under the name of revisionism, also made itself evident in the theory of women's emancipation. Edmund Fischer's conception of the woman question, first published in 1905, represented the application of revisionism to the problems of women's liberation.

The emergence of a left wing, right wing and centre faction within the Party concealed the fact, until the outbreak of the war, that the socialist theory was rapidly being undermined by the relative prosperity of the working class, which gave rise to the illusion that class antagonisms were being attenuated, and by the cooperation of the working-class movement's leading organs with the institutions of the bourgeoisie.

The Party split in 1917 brought these underlying antagonisms to light. For a short time after the war, Social Democracy held the reins of power, but because of its irresolute attitude to the transformation of society, it soon had to surrender them to the representatives of the bourgeoisie. The Demobilization Decrees, designed to effect the 'smoothest possible' transfer of military personnel into industry, proved to be an instrument forcing women out of production, into which they had been drawn in large numbers during the war. The men forced women to be dismissed, and the antagonism between the sexes, which was meant to have been abolished by the implementation of women's suffrage, broke out anew. The Party was unable to influence economic developments, and did not criticize them from the point of the theory of emancipation, but at the same time it tried to rescue its claim to be feminist. Symptomatic of this process was the ideology of social work.

The Communists took over the theory of women's emancipation which had been renounced by the Social Democrats. The Bolshevik Revolution tried to put it into practice on a grand scale. Since that time, Soviet development has undergone two fundamental stages. At first, the Revolution gave women absolute equality with men. In the initial years, the greatest possible freedom governed sexual relations. There was a protracted discussion on the new sexual morality, and Lenin intervened to utter a sharp condemnation of licentiousness, which he termed the 'liberation of the flesh'. The tenor of his criticism anticipated the subsequent clamp-down. At this time separation involved a simple official procedure possible at the request of either party; unregistered marriages were given equal status with registered ones. All jobs were declared open to women and contraceptives were made readily available. Abortion was permitted, and the setting-up of children's crèches encouraged. The principle that all relations between sexes were a private matter was still anchored in the Russian marriage code of 1927. The positive regulations above all concerned the protection of the mother's interests and the equal rights of both married partners with respect to children and property. At the outset, women's liberation from housework by means of centralized institutions for assistance had been an end in itself, but the ruthless recruitment of women workers in the course of the subsequent process of forced industrialization degraded women's liberation to a pretext for their exploitation.

The introduction of the Five Year Plans saw the rise of so-called 'socialist competition', which even affected married couples and which squeezed the most extreme performance out of women. A reactionary development also took place in family legislation. Separation was made more difficult, the regulations concerning the interruption of pregnancy were made more strict, and the 'free love' of the post-war years was transformed into a rigorous sexual morality which subordinated sexual relations to the requirements of 'socialist construction'. In the context of the Stalinist policy of socialism in one country women's equality in the Soviet Union proved to be, not the realization of women's liberation, but the necessary precondition for the industrialization and the collectivization of agriculture in an under-developed economy. Even the communal kitchens, child care centres and centralized households, which ought to have helped women to liberate themselves from unproductive and stupefying housework, were set up for the sole purpose of being able to exploit female labour to the full in the economy. In 1930, the Women's Committees of the Communist Party were dissolved on the grounds that they had outlived their usefulness. By this means the emancipation of women was neutralized in the same way as it had been in Germany by the implementation of women's suffrage. The small number of women among Party cadres and the relatively meagre women's representation on local committees and legislative bodies, proved that women's political influence lagged behind their participation in the process of production and that their equality with men was only a fact with respect to their exploitation as workers. The state's efforts to increase the birth rate conflicted, just as it did under National Socialism, with industry's need for women workers. The ideal of the 'mother of heroes' stood side by side with that of the 'shock worker'. The liberation of women in the Soviet Union admittedly led to a much more far-reaching abolition of male privileges than capitalism was able to achieve, but at the same time it led to the total subordination of women as workers and as mothers to the purposes of production in a manner that capitalism had long ago abandoned.[2]

In capitalist society, the revolutionary effect of female labour was limited to the achievement of women's legal equality and hence to the realization of the demands of the bourgeois women's movement. The women who were drawn into the process of production, however, were degraded into mere instruments of production.

It is impossible to give a critique of the socialist theory of women's liberation without taking into account the social conditions under which it arose and the history of the working-class movement as a whole. The two basic assumptions of this theory arose from certain necessary conditions of the social process in general and of the development of the socialist movement in particular. These basic assumptions can be described as follows:

1　The achievement of economic independence from the male is a precondition for women's liberation. The woman proletarian can only do this by herself going out to work. The capitalist tendency for female labour to increase, therefore, is simultaneously a tendency for the liberation of women from dependence on the male.

2　In order to prevent female labour from increasing women's misery because of its necessary side-effects under capitalism, legislation must be introduced to protect women workers. The woman worker will only be able to join in the proletariat's struggle for liberation if she is protected against blatant exploitation.

Both these basic assumptions have been verified by the development of the women's movement, the working-class movement and society. The question as to why women's emancipation has failed to come about despite this fact is answered by the socialist theory itself: it is because female labour and women's equality have been integrated into the existing society. The explosive force that was ascribed to them could only have been realized by a revolutionary working-class movement. The latter, however, fell victim to the same integrative process.

It is correct to say that by going out to work women have become more independent of men than they were under household conditions.

The male's primacy in the family was based on his role as

the foodgiver. To the extent that the woman now also contributes to the maintenance of life, his authority has dwindled. Women's growing share in the work force also ultimately brought women workers equal pay in jobs where they worked alongside men doing the same work. The independence afforded by their wages has its limits, however, as is shown by the fact that women workers remain predominantly dependent on inferior, simple, and for that reason poorly paid jobs. This is due both to the fact that occupational training for women has made only slow progress and to the 'functional theory' of female labour. A further important impediment to the extension of women's field of work lies in the existence of the bourgeois nuclear family. The married woman worker still has to accept a three-fold role as housewife, spouse and the person responsible for bringing up the children. The social organization of the female functions has not kept pace with the advance of female labour. It is not simply a matter of lagging behind social developments, however. The very same interests that make use of the woman as a producer also laid claim to her as a consumer, to the extent that they perpetuate and increase the needs of the individual household ideologically and thus tie the woman to a form of the family which comes into constant conflict with her career. If the working woman wants to get rid of housework, advertisements and the pressure to demonstrate her own status persuade her into buying all sorts of allegedly labour-saving devices. These then have to be acquired by the painful process of hire-purchase, and thus simultaneously force the woman to work and chain her even more securely to her household. If she seriously wants to train for a career, this goes against the feminine ideal propagated by the culture industry. On the other hand, many women cannot meet the standards of dress, cosmetics and equipment set up by this same culture industry unless they earn the money by their own work.

The obverse of women's acquisition of independence through work is the disintegration of the family. In the patriarchal order of the family, women had not merely suffered under the economically determined tutelage of the male. It also gave her, at least in certain strata of the bourgeoisie, a realm of security, intimacy, culture and even freedom relatively untouched by the conflicts of liberal society outside.

Women's deprivation of rights has dialectical consequences: Because of their wide-ranging isolation from the production process, they are cheated of opportunities to develop, but for this reason they are subjected less than the men to the dictates of competition. In the mind of the private person, this competition becomes the crucial factor in society, and also in the mutual hostility which inevitably always operates within this society. It is true that women are victims, but not of the kind that have their whole character sacrificed along with them.[3]

The very fact that women are unable to do what men achieve, namely the running of an inhuman society, means that the tyranny of the economy over people is repulsed at an important point.[4]

Women have been driven to work by their rebellion against male domination and by economic constraint. Formerly they were only subject to indirect social pressure, namely through the men's conformism to the liberal order, but now their work subjects them directly to the laws of material production. Although work turns women into wage-earners in the same way as male proletarians, they are able to defend themselves even less than the men against their dependence on the production apparatus, and on top of everything else the men confront them with a vested interest in the existing order. Women's oppression is reproduced in the world of work, but with the crucial difference that it is not mitigated by the love with which they were surrounded in the patriarchal family. Women's physical and intellectual weakness here turns directly into a source of discrimination against them. They have sacrificed the privilege of a non-purposeful existence without the compensation of the gratification of success, honour and power which is accorded to the men. Wherever they are not physically swallowed up by their work through exhaustion and over-exertion, and where they do not hide their suffering for fear of losing their job, women learn to treasure the value of their personality as reflected in the status. This is no longer compatible with devotion to the male. Instead, women who are conscious of their value could only enjoy a relationship based on exchange, which could be dissolved at will if the expected value in return was disappointing or was used up.

Marriage, relations between partners and their relationship to the children ought to have been a real test for the promise of the possibility of free development, or at least a place to heal the wounds that individuals suffer in public life as a result of their drive to expand; a place where individuality, liberated from the outside world, could stretch its limbs. But instead, the theatre of action for mutually exclusive individual interests is now removed even further into the inner sphere of the home and in fact becomes, as it were, the model for the general course of life, which is characterized by the alienation and seclusion of isolated people.[5]

It was thought that the introduction of women to the process of production would help them emancipate themselves, but in fact it has only made them wage-labourers, and the extreme division of labour has deprived their work of all its individual features making it a routine devoid of meaning and indifferent to the individuality of the worker. Dependence on the business trends of capitalism has forced women into rivalry with one another and with men. Female labour has neither wiped out traditional male privileges nor brought women liberation beyond the disposal over their wages, and even in this sphere they are not free. The work with which they have to buy themselves free from male tutelage exposes them to the universal hostility of their rivals and the superior competitiveness of the men. Although female labour serves to give women equal rights in capitalism, this merely obscures the fact that social equality continues. Even women's equal rights prove illusory when economic crises swell the ranks of the industrial reserve army and men demand more jobs.

There was undoubtedly a connexion, already clearly evident before the First World War, between the increase in female membership of Social Democracy and the trade unions on the one hand, and the increase in female labour on the other. But both this and the improvements in workers' protection and social legislation were merely necessary preconditions for women's liberation, not sufficient ones. They only realized emancipation as far as this was possible at all on the basis of a capitalist society. The implementation of women's legal equality with men after the 1918 Revolution was merely a consequence of the preceding development of female labour. Legal equality was also introduced in those countries where Social Democracy did not become the Government but where female labour had nonetheless reached large proportions. To that extent the socialist theory of women's emancipation had rightly seen that female labour and legal equality were preconditions for emancipation. It was wrong to assume, however, that female labour would automatically be converted into women's political, and particularly socialist activity, as Clara Zetkin had done when she wrote:

F

The economic development, which subjects the proletarian woman to the same exploitation as the men of her class, takes these female wage slaves who have apathetically accepted their fate and forges them into steel-hard fighters against the capitalists and their state and social order. In the economic and political struggle, therefore, the woman proletarian is changed from an obstructive to a driving force.[6]

Female labour itself could not have such an effect. Women workers would first need to become members of a revolutionary socialist women's movement, and this in turn presupposed the existence of a revolutionary working-class movement. Before the First World War, however, the radical wing of the Social Democratic women's movement increasingly found itself in conflict with the Party, for the latter was already feeling the effect of the dialectic of the rise and decline of the working-class movement. For special reasons arising from the discrimination of women even within the Party, a section of the women's movement clung to the old socialist theory, but the workers' movement had already submitted to the influence of revisionist thought. Social Democracy's behaviour during and after the war clearly showed that the working-class movement no longer strove for a fundamental alteration of society. Female labour, however, was thereby deprived of its revolutionary effect.

The further development of women's liberation was henceforth determined by the fact that while the necessary preconditions had been fulfilled, they were rendered insufficient by the continuance of the capitalist system. Women's emancipation therefore proceeded according to the laws of this society. The difference between the legal sphere, in which legal equality had been implemented, and the economy, which was not regulated by this formal equality and in which women's inequality and their position as mere instruments of production survived along with class relations, formed the insurpassable barrier to the further development of women's liberation.

(Emancipation was) warped by the continuation of traditional society. Little could be more symptomatic of the disintegration of the working class movement than the fact that it took no notice of this. The admission of women to every possible type of supervized activity conceals the fact of their continuing dehumanization. In the large enterprise they remained what they had been in the family—objects. We must not only bear in mind their miserable day at work and their life at home, where the isolated working conditions of the household are retained in the midst of the industrial ones against all reason. We must also remember the women themselves. Eagerly, and without any impulse to the contrary, they reflect their domination and identify with it. Instead of solving the woman question, male society has extended its principle to such an extent that the victims cannot even raise the question any more.[7]

It was not the inadequacy of socialist theory that was responsible for the failure to achieve women's complete emancipation, but the working-class movement's abandonment of its revolutionary goal. The theory had made it quite clear that equal rights were not identical with women's liberation. As early as 1892, Clara Zetkin had written in *Die Gleichheit*:

In view of the class situation, it is not enough for women to be emancipated from the male. A glance at the conditions of their male comrades tells the women proletarians that social liberation does not come merely through the possession of social and political rights, and that these rights are only a means to the end, not the end itself of their struggle for emancipation. The liberation of women workers does not consist merely in obtaining equality with the male world within the present society. Rather, the existing social order must be abolished in its entirety, for the economic and property relations of this society are the root of both class and sexual slavery.[8]

It was thus not the theory which was responsible for the wrong development of women's liberation, and in view of the fact that female labour would inevitably increase it was senseless to resist it. Nonetheless, it should be noted that proletarian anti-feminism, which from the very start opposed the idea of women being liberated as a result of their involvement in the capitalist process of production, ultimately proved to be more correct, in a sense, than the socialist theory. For the Socialists' hopes, which pointed beyond the existing social conditions, did not come to fulfilment. The revolutionary potential that female labour gave to the Social Democratic Party before 1914 was swallowed up in the reformist working-class movement, which failed to shatter the foundations of the capitalist system. It failed to turn the women who had been liberated from the narrow confines of the home and male domination into fighters for the class struggle, and instead completely subordinated their work to the need for practical life and utility which capitalism had spread over social relations and from which women had at least partly been exempt under household conditions. The survival of capitalism did not permit the dialectic, which might have been released by female labour, to come into effect. Admittedly, proletarian anti-feminism did not have any precise ideas about the real preconditions for female labour, but it was conscious of the fact that under the given circumstances it was not in the interests of the working class for women to have jobs. The socialist theory replied to this argument by pointing to the inevitable spread and the revolutionary effect of female labour.

While, on the one hand, the distrust of female labour was based on the correct insight that nothing good could come from the existing order, it displayed, on the other, the limits of a consciousness which does not think of the day after tomorrow because it does not know how it will survive the morrow, and which pusillanimously allows itself to be impressed into conformity by the might of the existing order. By accustoming itself to thinking in the categories of the ruling system, proletarian anti-feminism also blinded itself to the prospect of emancipation opened up by socialist theory. It based itself on facts that socialist theory wished to get beyond. By this means it did the women both justice and injustice: justice, in the sense that it wished to preserve them from the misery of exploitation, which it was however powerless to do, and injustice, in the sense that it bore this impotence with resignation and kept women, seemingly for their own sakes, away from the world of alienated labour in which they might have become aware of the possibility of a better society. By this means, however, it banished women's liberation once and for all into the realm of utopia. The truth inherent in the attitude of proletarian anti-feminism towards women's liberation consisted in the fact that it considered it to be impossible under capitalist relations of production. The consequence was that they resisted female labour.

The positive assessment of female labour by socialist theory derived from the fact that it thought it was possible to involve women proletarians in the anti-capitalist movement. It did of course have this effect, but the revolutionary consequences failed to come about because the working-class movement allowed its achievements to dissuade it from the goal of a socialist society and to rest content with winning its day-to-day, and far too minimal, demands. There is an intimate connexion between proletarian anti-feminism and revisionism, just as there is between radical women's emancipation and orthodox socialist theory. The defeat of the socialist women's movement was simultaneously the defeat of socialism as a whole, while the victory of reformism brought the views of proletarian anti-feminism to validity within the working-class movement. If the reformist theory was ultimately proved right and the socialist theory wrong, this happened precisely at the expense of the survival of the old system. Without socialism, the possible alternatives for the solution of the woman question are both equally depressing: either the women will adapt to the process of production, in which men maintain their former domination, or they will remain apart from it in the domestic sphere, swallowed up by the pressure to consume, by which society keeps itself going, and oppressed by economic dependence on the male.

> Hope cannot aim at making the mutilated social character of women identical to the mutilated social character of men; rather, its goal must be a state in which the face of the grieving woman disappears simultaneously with that of the bustling capable man, a state in which all that survives the disgrace of the difference between the sexes is the happiness that difference makes possible.[9]

References

The following abbreviations have been used in the footnotes:

Proceedings: Proceedings of the SPD Party Conference, held at . . . (The place of publication is Berlin in the same year: otherwise place and year are given)

Statistical Yearbook: Statistical Yearbook for the German Empire

Yearbook: Yearbook of German Social Democracy, Berlin . . .

Chapter 1
1 J. Kuczynski, *Die Geschichte der Lage der Arbeiter in Deutschland von 1789 bis in die Gegenwart*, 6th rev ed, Berlin 1954, vol 1, *1789 bis 1870*, pp 65, 161ff, 188.
2 F. Mehring, *Geschichte der deutschen Sozialdemokratie*, 2nd rev ed, Stuttgart 1903, vol 2, p 96.
3 L. Braun, *Die Frauenfrage*, Leipzig 1901, p 222. J. Kuczynski, *op cit*, p 72.
4 Cf H. Lion, *Zur Soziologie der Frauenbewegung*, Berlin 1926, p 28ff.
5 Marx's and Engels's statements on questions concerning women are brought together in R. Jaeckel, *Die Stellung des Sozialismus zur Frauenfrage im 19. Jahrhundert*, Dissertation, Potsdam 1904.

Chapter 2
1 Cf W. Schroeder, *Handbuch der sozialdemokratischen Parteitage*, vol 1, Munich 1910, p 463.
2 K. Marx, 'Critique of the Gotha Programme', in Marx and Engels, *Selected Works* (1 vol edition), London 1968, pp 317ff. Quote from p 322.
3 H. Lion, *Zur Soziologie der Frauenbewegung*, Berlin 1926, p 26.
4 L. Otto, *Das Recht der Frauen auf Erwerb*, Hamburg 1866, p 103.
5 In 1863 there were 104 workers' educational associations, 368 evangelical youth clubs and 188 catholic apprentices clubs. Added to this was a constantly growing number of groups affiliated to the Lassallean Workers' Association. Cf Mehring, *op cit*, vol 1, p 11.
6 *Bericht über die Verhandlungen des 3. Vereinstages deutscher Arbeitervereine zu Stuttgart, 3-5 September 1865*, Nürnberg 1865, pp 47-48.
7 *ibid*, p 49.
8 *ibid*, p 50.

9   *ibid*, p 51.
10   *ibid*, p 51.
11   H. Lion, *op cit*, p 14.
12   Cf *Die ersten deutschen Sozialistenkongresse*, Frankfurt/M 1906, p 33f.
13   Cf Mehring, *op cit*, vol 1, p 171.
14   *Der Vorbote*, 1866, Geneva 1868, p 44.
15   *The Communist Manifesto*, in *Selected Works*, *op cit*, p 38.
16   *ibid*, p 50.
17   *ibid*, p 42.
18   *Der Vorbote*, 1866, p 149.
19   *ibid*, p 151.
20   *ibid*, p 152.
21   *ibid*.
22   Cf Engels, 'Socialism: Utopian and Scientific', German edition Frankfurt/M 1946, p 4.
23   *Der Vorbote*, 1867, Geneva 1867, p 184.
24   *Der Vorbote*, 1868, Geneva, p 40. The *Vorbote* does not give a verbatim report.
25   Cf footnote 14 of this Chapter.
26   *Der Vorbote*, 1868, p 41.
27   *ibid*, p 54.
28   *Der Vorbote*, 1866, p 44.
29   *ibid*, p 151.
30   Marx, *Capital*, vol 1, Moscow 1959, pp 394ff, 489-90.
31   Cf R. Jaeckel, *op cit*, p 127.

Chapter 3

1   *Protokoll des Allgemeinen Deutschen Sozialdemokratischen Arbeiterkongresses, Eisenach 7-9 August 1869*, Leipzig 1869, p 33.
2   H. Lion, *op cit*, p 29.
3   O. Baader *Bericht für die Erste Internationale Konferenz sozialistischer Frauen*, Stuttgart 1909, p 13.
4   *Proceedings*, (*op cit* footnote 1 above), p 37.
5   W. Schröder, *op cit*, p 37.
6   H. Lion, *op cit*, p 28.
7   *ibid*, p 29.
8   *Der Vorbote*, 1871, Geneva 1871, p 184.
9   Women were not given the freedom of association until the enactment of the 1908 Combination Laws. Cf C. Zetkin, *Bericht an die zweite Internationale Konferenz sozialistischer Frauen in Kopenhagen vom 26-27 August 1910*, Stuttgart, nd, p 1.
10   O. Baader, *op cit*, p 5.
11   *ibid*, p 8.
12   Cf Hilde Lion, *op cit*, p 73ff.
13   *ibid*, p 30.
14   *Der Volksstaat*, 1873, no 63, Leipzig 1873.
15   'Protokoll des Vereinigungskongresses der Sozialdemokraten Deutschlands zu Gotha', in *Die ersten Sozialistenkongresse*, *op cit*, p 69.
16   *ibid*, p 73.
17   *ibid*, p 75.
18   *ibid*, p 98.
19   *ibid*, p 109.

20   *ibid*, p 111.
21   *ibid*, p 112.
22   Marx, 'Critique of the Gotha Programme', in Marx and Engels, *Selected Works*, p 330.
23   Bebel, *Women and Socialism*, New York 1971, p 180.
24   *ibid*, p 293.
25   W. Schröder, *op cit*, pp 39-40.
26   *ibid*, p 41.
27   E. Bernstein, *Dokumente des Sozialismus*, Berlin 1902-1904, vol 1, p 84, and *Neue Zeit*, 1890/91, Stuttgart 1890, pp 508-509.
28   Cf *Rote Feldpost*, in *Archiv für Geschichte des Sozialismus etc*, vol 3, 1912, p 549.
29   Bebel, *op cit*, pp 150, 154, 178.
30   H. Lion, *op cit*, pp 35-38.
31   *ibid*.
32   Cf H. Cunow, *Die Marx'sche Geschichts-, Gesellschafts- und Staatstheorie*, vol 2, Berlin 1921, p 84.
33   'Zur Kritik der Engels'schen Urgeschichtskonstruktion', cf *ibid*, pp 138-142.
34   Cf Engels, *Der Ursprung der Familie, des Privateigentums und des Staates*, Berlin 1954, pp vi, 31.
35   K. Kautsky, *Die materialistische Geschichtsauffassung*, Berlin 1927, vol 1, pp 323-324.
36   Cf Engels, *op cit*, pp 50, 53, 58.

Chapter 4

1   *Protokoll des Internationalen Arbeiterkongresses, Paris 14-20 Juli 1889*, tr W. Liebknecht, Nürnberg 1890, p 81.
2   *ibid*, p 84.
3   *ibid*, p 83.
4   *ibid*, p 122.
5   *ibid*, p 83.
6   Marx, *Capital*, vol 1, p 395.
7   *Neue Zeit*, 1888, p 124.
8   E. Dolléans and M. Crozier, *Mouvements ouvrier et socialiste, 1750-1918 (Angleterre, France, Allemagne, Etats Unis)*, Paris 1950, and Kuczynski, *op cit*, p 71.
9   Cf J. Kuczynski, *op cit*, p 224.
10   Cf A. Bebel, *op cit*, p 181.
11   L. Braun, *Die Frauen und die Politik*, Berlin 1903, p 39.
12   Cf C. Zetkin, *Die Arbeiterinnen- und Frauenfrage der Gegenwart*, Berlin 1889.
13   Cf M. Juchacz, *Sie lebten für eine bessere Welt*, Berlin 1955, pp 34-35, and L. Braun, *Die Frauenfrage*, Leipzig, 1901, pp 434-435.
14   *Proceedings*: Halle 1890, Berlin 1890, p 48.
15   Cf L. Braun, *op cit*, p 451.
16   *Proceedings*: Halle 1890, pp 196-197.
17   F. Mehring, *op cit*, Vol 4, pp 319, 321, 325.
18   E. Ihrer, *Die Arbeiterinnen im Klassenkampf*, Hamburg 1898, p 27.
19   H. Lion, *op cit*, pp 32-33.
20   Literature on the beginnings of the women workers' movement: A. Berger, *Die zwanzigjährige Arbeiterinnenbewegung Berlins und ihr Ergebnis*, Berlin 1889.

E. Bernstein, *Geschichte der Berliner Arbeiterbewegung*, Berlin 1910, Part 3.

L. Braun, 'Die Arbeiterinnenbewegung', in *Die Frauenfrage*, pp 431-462.

E. Ihrer, *Die Organisation der Arbeiterinnen Deutschlands*, Berlin 1893.

E. Ihrer, *Die Arbeiterinnen im Klassenkampf*, Hamburg 1898.

J. Joos, *Die sozialdemokratische Frauenbewegung*, München-Gladbach 1912.

E. Lüders, *Arbeiterinnenorganisation und Frauenbewegung*, 2nd edition, Leipzig 1904.

21   *Proceedings*: Erfurt 1891, p 5.

22   *Neue Zeit* 1890/91, vol 2, p 181.

23   Cf *Die Gleichheit*, 1893, no 19.

24   *Verhandlungen und Beschlüsse des Internationalen Arbeiterkongresses zu Brüssel*, 16-22 August 1891, Berlin 1893, p 32.

25   *ibid*, p 33.

26   *Proceedings*: Breslau 1895, Paragraph 9, No 1, of the Organizational Statute, p 7.

27   Cf *Proceedings*: Frankfurt 1894, pp 174-175, and W. Schröder, *op cit*, vol 2, p 161.

28   *Proceedings*: Mainz 1900, p 7.

29   H. Lion, *op cit*, pp 96-97, and J. Joos, *op cit*, p 29. *Proceedings*: Hannover 1899, p 66.

30   *Proceedings*: Gotha 1896, p 160.

31   H. Lion, *op cit*, pp 96-97 and Table I of this dissertation.

32   *Proceedings*: Gotha 1896, p 40.

33   *Proceedings*: Stuttgart 1898, p 131.

34   Cf *ibid* and *Proceedings*: Munich 1902, pp 306-307.

35   Cf W. Schröder, *op cit*, vol 1, p 181, *Sozialistische Monatshefte*, 1924, p 652, and the section headed 'Debate on the Press' in Chapter 8 of the present dissertation.

36   *Protokoll des Internationalen Sozialistischen Arbeiterkongresses*, Zurich 1894, p 97.

37   Cf Marx, *Capital*, vol 1, p 458 and Bebel, *op cit*, pp 160ff.

38   *Proceedings*: Cologne 1893, pp 25, 27, 28, 246 and *Proceedings*: Frankfurt 1894, p 50.

39   A. Blos, *Die Frauenfrage im Lichte des Sozialismus*, Dresden 1930, p 34 and *Proceedings*: Frankfurt 1894, p 58.

40   *Proceedings*: Breslau 1895, pp 18, 20, 197-200, 204, 206.

41   *Protokoll des internationalen Sozialistischen Arbeiter- und Gewerkschafts-kongresses, London 27 July bis 1 August 1896*, Berlin 1896, p 29.

42   *Proceedings*: Gotha 1896, pp 160ff and p 183.

43   *ibid*, pp 173-175.

44   H. Lion, *op cit*, p 59, cf L. Braun, *op cit*, p 445f.

45   The fiscal report of the *IG Metall* (the German Metal Workers Union) for 1965-67 reveals that on 31.12.1967 the wages of the lowest wage group, which predominantly consisted of women, amounted to 70 per cent to 75 per cent of those for the wage group for simple technical jobs. (p 135)
The report comments: 'Although there are no longer any groups in our wage agreements which are exclusively for men or for women, we still find wage groups for so-called physical work. Normally physical strain is taken to mean only muscular strain. It has long been undisputed, however, that precisely the so-called light physical jobs demand a high level of skill and dexterity. Besides this, they have to be performed in very short time-cycles; in addition, therefore, demands are made on the workers' concentration. All these things require unprecedented efforts on the part of the worker. The monotony of the work

and the one-sided nature of the effort entail substantial aggravations.
Up to the present, such insights have not been reflected adequately in wages.
Jobs which are predominantly performed by women are still regarded as
physically light. The lowest wage groups are hence likewise preserved for
women.' (p 303)
On this point, see also Olaf Radke and Wilhelm Rathert, *Gleich-Berechtigung?*,
Frankfurt/Main 1964.

46   Sources for Table 1:

a   *Neue Zeit*, 1891/92, vol 1, p 57.

b   A. Geyer, *Die Frauenerwerbsarbeit in Deutschland*, Jena 1924, p 9.

c   *Die Gleichheit*, 1908/09, no 25.

d   *Archiv für die Geschichte des Sozialismus etc*, vol 4, Leipzig 1913, p 485.

e   *Bericht der Vertrauensperson der Genossinnen Deutschlands für die Zeit von August 1905 bis Ende Juli 1906*, pp 70, 72, 73.

f   *Bericht des Parteivorstandes der SPD an den Internationalen Sozialistenkongress in Kopenhagen (1910) über die Tätigkeit der Partei seit dem Stuttgarter Kongress* (1907), no place, no date, pp 33-35.

g   W. Schröder, *op cit*, vol 2, pp 139 and 181.

h   J. Joos, *op cit*, pp 29 and 36.

i   *Proceedings*: Essen 1907, p 216, list of persons present.

j   *Proceedings*: Magdeburg 1910, list of persons present.

k   *Proceedings*: Halle 1890, list of persons present.

l   *Proceedings*: Erfurt 1891, list of persons present.

m   *Proceedings*: Breslau 1895, list of persons present.

n   *Proceedings*: Stuttgart 1898, list of persons present.

o   *Proceedings*: Hannover 1899, list of persons present.

p   *Proceedings*: Manheim 1906, list of persons present.

q   *Proceedings*: Nürnberg 1908, list of persons present.

r   *Proceedings*: Leipzig 1909, list of persons present.

s   *Proceedings*: Jena 1911, list of persons present.

t   *Proceedings*: Chemnitz 1912, list of persons present.

u   *Proceedings*: Jena 1913, list of persons present.

v   H. Lion, *op cit*, p 148.

47   Cf W. Sombart, *Der proletarische Sozialismus*, Jena 1925, vol 2, p 111.

48   Cf Bebel, 'Zwei literarische Erzeugnisse über die Frauenfrage', in *Neue Zeit*, 20, 1902, vol 1, p 293ff.

49   Cf *Proceedings*: Dresden 1903, p 158ff.

50   Cf *ibid*, p 258.

51   M. Juchacz, *op cit*, p 60.

52   Cf *Proceedings*: Munich 1902, Women's Conference, p 294 and 300; M. Juchacz, *op cit*, p 60; L. Braun, *Frauenarbeit und Hauswirtschaft*, Berlin 1901.

53   Cf *Die Gleichheit*, 1900, no 20.

54   *Proceedings*: Munich 1902, Women's Conference, p 288ff and 23-24.

55   *Bericht der Vertrauensperson etc*, p 68.

56   C. Zetkin, *Zur Frage des Frauenwahlrechts*, Berlin 1907, p 53.

57   Cf Engels, *Die englische Zehnstundenbill*, pp 386-389.

58   L. Zietz, *Die Frauen und die Politik*, Berlin 1912, pp 9ff.

59   H. Lion, *op cit*, p 98.

60   *Bericht der Vertrauensperson etc*, pp 70ff.

61   *Protokoll des Internationalen Sozialistenkongresses, Stuttgart 18-24 August 1907*, Berlin 1907, pp 41ff.

62   *Bericht des Parteivorstandes der SPD etc*, p 27.

63   *Proceedings*: Nürnberg 1908, Women's Conference.
64   Cf W. Schröder, *op cit*, vol 2, p 145.
65   *Proceedings*: Stuttgart 1898, p 112.
66   *Proceedings*: Mainz 1900, p 185 and 138.
67   *Proceedings*: Gotha 1896, p 170.
68   Cf *Proceedings*: Stuttgart 1898, pp 112, 122, 131.
69   *Proceedings*: Stuttgart 1898, p 114.
70   *Proceedings*: Gotha 1896, p 170.
71   Cf F. Mehring, *op cit*, vol 4, p 184.
72   H. Langerhans, *Partei und Gewerkschaft*, Dissertation, Frankfurt/M 1931, unpublished manuscript, p 30.
73   Cf *ibid*, pp 30-31.
74   Cf *ibid*, pp 34-35.
75   *ibid*, p 44.
76   Cf J. Kuczynski, *op cit*, p 158.
77   H. Langerhans, *op cit*, p 86.
78   Cf *ibid*, pp 61ff.
79   *ibid*, p 69.
80   *ibid*, p 86.
81   *ibid*, p 81.
82   On the bureaucratization of the working-class movement cf R. Michels, *Political Parties: A Sociological Study of the Oligarchical Tendencies of Modern Democracy*, London 1915; L. Kofler, *Marxistischer oder ethischer Sozialismus*, Bovenden b. Göttingen 1955, the Chapter entitled 'Volkstribun oder Bürokrat'; K. D. Bracher, *Die Auflösung der Weimarer Republik*, Stuttgart-Düsseldorf 1955, pp 74-77.
83   Paul Sering, quoted in H. Matthias, *Sozialdemokratie und Nation*, Stuttgart 1952, p 53.
84   H. Langerhans, *op cit*, p 92.
85   R. Michels, *op cit*, Part 3, Ch 1, pp 224-225.
86   On pre-war Social Democracy see also:
K. Mandelbaum, *Die Erörterungen unnerhalb der deutschen Sozialdemokratie über das Problem des Imperialismus*, Dissertation, Frankfurt/M, 1927, pp 5-18; K. F. Brockschmidt, *Die Deutsche Sozialdemokratie bis zum Fall des Sozialistengesetzes*, Dissertation, Frankfurt/M-Stuttgart 1929; H. Heidegger, *Die Deutsche Sozialdemokratie und der nationale Staat* (Vol 25 of the *Göttinger Bausteine zur Geschichtswissenschaft*), Berlin-Frankfurt/M 1956.

Chapter 5
1   O. K. Flechtheim, *Die KPD in der Weimarer Republik*, Offenbach/M 1948, p 9. New edition Frankfurt/M 1969.
2   *ibid*.
3   R. Fischer, *Stalin and German Communism*, London 1948, p 11.
4   H. Lion, *op cit*, p 156; cf W. Zepler, 'Unser Frauenzentralorgan', in *Sozialistische Monatshefte*, 1915, vol 2, p 693.
5   *Proceedings*: Leipzig 1931, p 284.
6   *ibid*, p 99.
7   M. Juchacz, *op cit*, p 56.
8   L. Preller, *Sozialpolitik in der Weimarer Republik*, Stuttgart 1949, pp 29, 31 and 7.
9   Cf *Die Gleichheit*, 1912/13, no 13, 14, 77, 23, 24.
10   *ibid*, no 25.
11   Cf *Die Gleichheit*, 1914/15, no 15.

12   *Proceedings*: Essen 1907, p 270.

13   Cf *Die Gleichheit*, 1914/15, no 24.

14   Cf *ibid*, no 17, 1916/17, no 12-17; cf also H. Lion, *op* cit, p 157 and *Proceedings*: Würzburg 1917, p 309.

15   Cf *Die Gleichheit*, 1916/17, no 10.

16   *ibid*, no 16.

17   *ibid*, no 18.

18   *ibid*, Special Supplement.

19   A. Rosenberg, *A History of the German Republic*, London, 1936, p 18.

20   *Die Gleichheit*, 1919, no 20.

21   Cf Table 2 below.

22   Cf Table 3 below.

23   Cf Preface to no 1 of *Gewerkschaftliche Frauenarbeit*, vol 1, 1916.

24   Cf H. Lion, *op cit*, p 157.

25   *Gewerkschaftliche Frauenarbeit*, 1917, no 11.

26   Cf *Proceedings*: Weimar 1919, p 19.

27   *ibid*, p 463.

28   *ibid*, p 471.

29   *Gewerkschaftliche Frauenarbeit*, 1917, no 10.

30   *Proceedings*: Würzburg 1917, p 439.

31   Kuczynski's figure of 700,000 for the increase in women workers refers only to enterprises with at least 10 employees.

32   J. Kuczynski, *op cit*, Part 2, p 118.

33   F. Stampfer, *Die ersten 14 Jahre der deutschen Republik*, 2nd impression Offenbach/M 1947, pp 21-22. A sharp rebuff for 'war socialism' is given by Johannes Kämpfer in his book, *Kriegssozialismus in Theorie und Praxis*, Bern 1915; Cf also H. Peus, 'Der Sozialismus und der sogenannte Kriegssozialismus', *Sozialistische Monatshefte* 1917, vol 1.

34   Cf *Proceedings*: Würzburg 1917, p 489-490.

35   W. Zepler, *Die Frauen und der Krieg*, Berlin 1916, p 7; W. Zepler, 'Der Krieg und die Frau', in *Sozialistische Monatshefte*, 1914, vol 2, p 1184; G. Hanna, 'Die Förderung der Frauenerwerbsarbeit durch den Krieg', in *Sozialistische Monatshefte*, 1915, vol 2, p 872; A. Blos, *Kommunale Frauenarbeit im Kriege*, Berlin 1917; P. Umbreit, 'Die Frauenarbeit vor und nach dem Krieg', in *Sozialistische Monatshefte*, 1918, vol 1, p 532.

36   Cf E. Eyck, *A History of the Weimar Republic*, 1, Cambridge Mass 1962, p 61.

37   Cf *Proceedings*: Weimar 1919, p 21.

38   *ibid*, p 465.

39   M. Juchacz, *op cit*, p 112; cf *Gewerkschaftliche Frauenarbeit*, 1919, no 3.

40   Cf M. Juchacz, *op cit*, pp 54, 60, 70.

41   Fr. Stampfer, *op cit*, pp 302-303.

42   Cf *Die Verfassung des Deutschen Reiches vom 11 August 1919*, 3rd edition, Berlin-Leipzig 1927, Articles 17, 22, 109, 119, and 128.

43   Cf *Grundgesetz für die Bundesrepublik Deutschland vom 23 Mai 1949*, Reclam edition, Stuttgart 1953, Article 3; *Verfassung der Deutschen Demokratischen Republik*, Berlin 1949, Articles 7, 18, 30 and 32.

Chapter 6

1   L. Preller, *op cit*, pp 6, 8, 24.

2   A. Rosenberg, *op cit*, pp 39-40.

3   Cf *Gewerkschaftliche Frauenarbeit*, 1918, nos 12 and 15.

4   Cf *ibid*, nos 21 and 23; *Proceedings*: Würzburg 1917, p 442f.

5   L. Preller, *op cit*, pp 53, 54.
6   *ibid*, p 281.
7   *Proceedings*: Würzburg 1917, pp 155-56.
8   *Proceedings*: Weimar 1919, pp 486-489.
9   J. Kuczynski, *op cit*, Part 2, p 230.
10   *Die Gleichheit*, 1919, no 14.
11   Cf *ibid*, no 23 and 1920, no 1, cf *Proceedings*: Görlitz 1921, p 30.
12   Cf *Gewerkschaftlichen Frauenarbeit*, 1919, no 2.
13   *Proceedings*: Kassel 1920, p 115.
14   J. Kuczynski, *op cit*, p 230.
15   G. Hanna, 'Die Arbeiterin in der Gewerkschaft', *Sozialistische Monats-
     hefte*, 1922, vol 1, p 509.
16   A. Rosenberg, *op cit*, p 39; cf L. Preller, *op cit*, p 295.
17   The following statistics are taken from: E. Ehehalt, *Die Deutsche Arbeits-
     losigkeit in der Nachkriegszeit*, Dissertation, Frankfurt/M-Gelnhausen 1932, pp
     15-17, 40-43, 45; W. Woytinsky, *Der deutsche Arbeitsmarkt*, Berlin 1930, Part
     1, pp 55-56, 72-75, 121ff; Part 2, Tables 32-35; *Statistical Yearbook* 1921/22—
     1933, statistics on the recipients of unemployment benefits.
18   Statement at the Munich Party Conference 1912, quoted in W. Schröder,
     op cit, vol 1, p 515.
19   E. Fischer, 'Die Frauenfrage', *Sozialistische Monatshefte*, 1905, vol 1,
     p 258.
20   Cf the discussion of Proudhon's theory of the family in R. Prigent, *op cit*,
     pp 88-97 and 147.
21   E. Fischer, 'Die Frauenfrage', p 259.
22   *ibid*, p 262.
23   Cf A. Geyer, *op cit*, p 9; A. Blos, *op cit*, pp 142 and 149.
24   Cf C. Zetkin, *Die Arbeiterinnen- und Frauenfrage der Gegenwart*, Berlin
     1889, pp 3-4.
25   E. Fischer, 'Die Frauenfrage', p 262.
26   Cf M. Komarowsky, 'Functional Analysis of Sex Roles', *American Socio-
     logical Review*, vol 15, pp 508-516; M. Komarowsky, *Women in the Modern
     World*, Boston 1953, p 53ff M. Mead, *Male and Female*, New York 1949, pp 8,
     160, 367.
27   E. Fischer, 'Die Frauenfrage', p 263.
28   *ibid*.
29   *ibid*, p 265-266.
30   E. Fischer, 'Die Familie', *Sozialistische Monatshefte*, 1905, vol 1, p 539.
31   Cf C. Zetkin, 'Aus Krähwinkel', *Die Gleichheit*, 1905, no 6.
32   Cf *Sozialistische Monatshefte*, 1905, vol 1, pp 443ff, 301ff, vol 2, pp
     1031ff, 1906, vol 1, pp 306ff.
33   E. Fischer, 'Tendenzen der Frauenarbeit', *Sozialistische Monatshefte*,
     1917, vol 2, p 545.
34   W. Zepler, *Sozialismus und Frauenfrage*, Berlin 1919, p 58.
35   *ibid*, p 64.
36   *ibid*, pp 69-77.

Chapter 7

1   Cf *Proceedings*: Weimar 1919, pp 465, 486 and 489.
2   Cf *Proceedings*: Kassel 1920, pp 68 and 115.
3   Cf *Proceedings*: Görlitz 1921, pp IV-VI.
4   Cf *Proceedings*: Heidelberg 1925, pp 8-9.
5   Cf *ibid*, Para 5, p 11; Para 8, p 12; Para 17, p 14; Para 22, p 15.

6   To some extent and in individual areas women had already previously enjoyed a limited right to vote; on this point cf G. Bremme, *Die politische Rolle der Frauen in Deutschland*, vol 4 of the series published by the UNESCO Institute for Social Sciences, Cologne-Göttingen 1956, p 24, footnote 2.

7   *ibid*, p 25.

8   Cf *Gewerkschaftliche Monatshefte*, 1919, no 3.

9   Cf *Die Gleichheit*, 1920, no 27.

10   *Proceedings*: Görlitz 1921, p 16.

11   *ibid*, p 186; cf *Proceedings*: Heidelberg 1925, p 345.

12   *Proceedings*: Berlin 1924, p 225.

13   *Proceedings*: Görlitz 1921, p 226.

14   *ibid*, p 46.

15   *Proceedings*: Berlin 1924, p 231.

16   *ibid*, p 232.

17   Cf G. Bremme, *op cit*, p 73.

18   M. Schneider, 'Die deutsche Wählerin', *Die Gesellschaft*, 1927, vol 2, pp 364-370.

19   Cf G. Bremme, *op cit*, p 29.

20   *ibid*, p 65, cf p 37.

21   Cf *ibid*, pp 72 and 77.

22   Cf *ibid*, pp 76-77.

23   Cf *ibid*, pp 220-221.

24   Cf *ibid*, p 64.

25   Cf *ibid*, p 69.

26   Sources for Table 2:

a   *Proceedings*: Görlitz 1921, pp 10 and 11.

b   *Proceedings*: Berlin 1924, National Women's Conference, p 16.

c   *Proceedings*: Heidelberg, p 39.

d   *Yearbook*, 1926, pp 25, 29.

e   *Yearbook*, 1927, pp 178, 181, 185.

f   *Proceedings*: Magdeburg 1929, p 44.

g   *Yearbook* 1930, p 201.

h   *Yearbook* 1931, p 109.

i   *Bericht der Vertrauensperson* etc, p 72.

j   *Bericht des Parteivorstandes der SPD* etc, pp 33-35.

k   W. Schröder, *op cit*, vol 2, p 239.

l   *Die Gleichheit* 1916/17, no 1.

m   *Proceedings*: Weimar 1919, p 54.

Figures whose source is not indicated were calculated by me on the basis of the available material.

27   *Proceedings*: Görlitz 1921, p 47.

28   Cf *ibid*, p 185.

29   *ibid*, p 184.

30   *Proceedings*: Heidelberg 1925, p 117.

31   A. Rosenberg, *op cit*, p 158.

32   Sources for Table 3:

a   W. Schröder, *op cit*, Vol 2, p 181.

b   *Proceedings*: Weimar 1919, p 36.

c   *Proceedings*: Görlitz 1921, p 41.

d   *Gewerkschaftliche Frauenarbeit*, 1917, no 11.

e   *Die Gleichheit*, 1922, no 3.

f   *Proceedings*: Berlin 1924, p 77.

g   *Proceedings*: Heidelberg 1925, pp 37, 67, 338.

h   *Proceedings*: Kiel 1927, p 318.
i   *Yearbook* 1928, p 146.
j   *Yearbook* 1931, p 126.
33   Cf M. Juchacz, *op cit*, p 102.
34   Cf *Proceedings*: Görlitz 1921, p 41.
35   Cf M. Juchacz, *op cit*, p 105.
36   *Proceedings*: Berlin 1925, pp 18-20.
37   Cf *Yearbook* 1928, p 147.
38   Cf *Proceedings*: Berlin 1924, p 262f.
39   *ibid*, p 233.
40   *ibid*, p 235; Cf *Proceedings*: Heidelberg 1925, p 165.
41   Cf *Proceedings*: Berlin 1924, p 237; also *Proceedings*: Magdeburg 1929, p 48.
42   Cf *Proceedings*: Kiel 1927, pp 305-306.
43   *Proceedings*: Berlin 1924, p 238.
44   *ibid*, p 231.
45   *Proceedings*: Heidelberg 1925, pp 334-335.
46   *Proceedings*: Magdeburg 1929, p 50; cf also *Proceedings*: Kiel 1927, pp 47-48.
47   *Proceedings*: Görlitz 1921, p 41.
48   *ibid*, p 30.
49   *ibid*, p 243.
50   *Proceedings*: Berlin 1924, pp 233-2 34.
51   Cf *Die Verfassung des Deutschen Reiches, op cit*, pp 296, 335.
52   *Proceedings*: Heidelberg 1925, p 168.
53   *ibid*, p 302.
54   *ibid*, p 308.
55   Cf *Sozialistische Monatshefte*, 1930, vol 2, p 920.
56   *Proceedings*: Leipzig 1931, p 284.
57   A. Blos, 'Der Fraueneinfluss bei den Wahlen', *Die Gleichheit*, 1920, no 27.
58   Cf *Proceedings*: Weimar 1919, pp 117-118 and *Proceedings*: Kiel 1927 p 48.
59   *Proceedings*: Görlitz 1921, p 385, cf also *Proceedings*: Kiel 1927, p 370.
60   *Proceedings*: Berlin 1924, p 239.
61   *ibid*, p 308.
62   *Proceedings*: Heidelberg 1925, p 333.
63   Cf *Proceedings*: Weimar 1919, pp 337, 505; also *Proceedings*: Heidelberg 1925, p 166.
64   *Proceedings*: Weimar 1919, p 15.
65   *Proceedings*: Görlitz 1921, p 13.
66   *Proceedings*: Magdeburg 1929, pp 238-239.
67   *Proceedings*: Görlitz 1921, p 73; also *Proceedings*: Weimar 1919, pp 126, 476.
68   *Proceedings*: Magdeburg 1929, p 238.
69   *ibid*, p 240.
70   *Proceedings*: Berlin 1924, p 224.
71   *Proceedings*: Heidelberg 1925, p 333; cf also *Yearbook* 1929, p 373.
72   Cf Table 2, p 116.
73   Sources for Table 4:
a   *Proceedings*: Görlitz 1921, p 36.
b   *ibid*, p 11.
c   *Proceedings*: Berlin 1924, p 19.

d   *Proceedings*: Heidelberg 1925, pp 60, 61.
e   *Proceedings*: Kiel 1927, p 312.
f   *Yearbook* 1930, p 212.
g   *Yearbook* 1930, p 212.
h   M. Schneider, in *Die Gesellschaft*, 1933, p 77.
The minutes of the Görlitz Party Conference in 1921 quote only 18 female
Members for the National Assembly. For the USPD Schneider quotes 3 in
1919, 9 in 1920; for the KPD in the first *Reichstag* 1920, 1, 2nd *Reichstag* 1924,
5, 3rd *Reichstag* 1924, 3, 4th *Reichstag* 1928, 3, 5th *Reichstag* 1930, 12, 6th
Reichstag 1932, 13, 7th *Reichstag* 1932, 13 female Members.
74   Cf *Proceedings*: Kiel 1927, p 312.
75   *Proceedings*: Görlitz 1921, National Women's Conference, p 17.
76   *ibid*, p 18.
77   *ibid*, p 17.
78   *ibid*.
79   *ibid*, p 10.
80   *Proceedings*: Heidelberg 1925, p 119.
81   *Proceedings*: Heidelberg 1925, p 47.
82   *Proceedings*: Görlitz 1921, National Women's Conference, p 43.
83   *ibid*, p 11.
84   *ibid*.
85   Cf *ibid*, p 10.
86   *ibid*, p 12.
87   *ibid*, p 14.
88   *ibid*, p 76.
89   Cf *Yearbook* 1928, p 152.
90   Cf *Yearbook* 1930, pp 226-227.
91   The concepts 'théorie fonctionelle' and 'politique du foyer' for the
situation described by me are taken from Duverger, *La Participation des Femmes
à la Vie politique,* quoted in Bremme, *op cit,* p 224.

Chapter 8

1   E. Ehehalt, *op cit*, p 44; L. Preller, *op cit*, p 124.
2   All figures quoted are from L. Preller, *op cit*, p 115-123.
3   S. Suhr, *Die weiblichen Angestellten*, Berlin 1930, pp 2, 10, 31, 47.
4   A. Siemsen, 'Die Berufslage der erwerbstätigen Frau', *Sozialistische Monats-
     hefte*, 1929, vol 2, pp 581, 582, 586.
5   *Proceedings*: Magdeburg 1929, pp 244, 220ff and *Yearbook* 1929 p 462.
6   Cf S. Suhr, *op cit*, p 10.
7   Cf *Proceedings*: Magdeburg 1929, p 268 and *Proceedings*: Leipzig 1931,
     p 284.
8   *Proceedings*: Magdeburg 1929, p 58.
9   Cf Table 2, p 116 above.
10   *Proceedings*: Leipzig 1931, p 249.
11   Sources for Table 5:
a   Cf sources for Table 1 above.
b   *Statistical Yearbook* 1921/22, p 457; 1932, p 436; 1924/25, p 403; 1926,
     p 466; 1927, p 513; 1928, p 594; 1929, p 496; 1930, p 576; 1932, p 556.
c   *Neue Zeit* 1922, vol 2, p 68.
12   Cf *Gewerkschaftliche Frauenzeitung*, 1925, no 9.
13   Cf *Yearbook* 1927, pp 189-191.
14   Cf *Yearbook* 1928, pp 144-150.
15   Sources for Table 6:

a   *Yearbook* 1926 p 32.
b   *Yearbook* 1928, p 147.
c   *Yearbook* 1930, p 221.
d   *Yearbook* 1931, p 124.
16   Cf *Gewerkschaftliche Frauenzeitung*, 1931, No 4.
17   Cf *Yearbook* 1931, pp 122-126.

Chapter 9
1   Cf Chapter 4 above.
2   Cf *Gewerkschaftliche Frauenzeitung*, 1926, no 7.
3   Cf *Sozialistische Monatshefte*, 1927, pp 718-720.
4   Cf *Sozialistische Monatshefte*, 1930, p 76.
5   Cf *Proceedings*: Magdeburg 1929, p 229 and *Yearbook* 1929, p 190.
6   Cf *Protokoll des 4 Kongresses der SAI und der 4. Internationalen Frauen-konferenz, Wien* 1931, Zurich 1932, p 180, and *Gewerkschaftliche Frauenarbeit*, 1930, nos 3 and 5.
7   J. Kuczynski, *op cit*, p 241, vol 1, Part 2.
8   *ibid*, p 252.
9   Cf L. Preller, *op cit*, pp 369ff, and K. L. Bracher, *op cit*, p 201.
10   C. Zetkin, 'Folgen des gesetzlichen Arbeiterinnenschutzes in wirtschaft-licher Beziehung', *Die Gleichheit*, 1893, no 20.
11   Cf *Proceedings*: Magdeburg 1929, p 268 and *Proceedings*: Leipzig 1931, p 284.
12   Cf A. Rosenberg, *op cit*, p 249.
13   *ibid*, p 275.
14   *ibid*, pp 285, 304.
15   *ibid*, p 305.
16   Cf *Yearbook* 1931, p 109.

Conclusion
1   Cf *Die Gleichheit* 1896, no 20, and 1897, no 16.
2   On female labour and emancipation in the Soviet Union of:
N. D. Aralowez, *Die Arbeit in der Industrie der UdSSR*, Berlin 1956.
F. Halle, *Die Frau in Sowjetrussland*, Berlin-Vienna-Leipzig 1932.
N. Popowa, *Die Gleichberechtigung der Frau, ihre Stellung in der Sowjetunion*, Berlin 1948.
R. Schlesinger, *Changing Attitudes in Soviet Russia—The Family*, 1st edition, London 1949.
3   L. Löwenthal, 'Das Individuum in der individualistischen Gesellschaft', *Zeitschrift für Sozialforschung*, vol V/1936, Paris 1936, no 3, p 349; cf also Horkheimer et al, *op cit*, p 63ff.
4   *ibid*, p 350.
5   *ibid*, p 330.
6   *Die Gleichheit*, 1897, no 16.
7   T. W. Adorno, *Minima Moralia*, Frankfurt/M 1964, p 115.
8   *Die Gleichheit*, 1892, no. 18.
9   T. W. Adorno, *Prisms*, London 1967, p 82.

Select Bibliography

Primary source material used by the author is referred to in the footnotes and is not listed separately here. The following list is merely one of secondary works cited in the footnotes. Where possible quotations have been traced to available English translations but most of the works referred to are not available in English.

T W Adorno	*Minima Moralia*, Frankfurt/M 1964
T W Adorno	*Prisms*, London 1967
N D Aralowez	*Die Arbeit der Frau in der Industrie der UdSSR*, Berlin 1956
A Bebel	*Women under Socialism* (Translated from the Original German of the 33rd Edition by Daniel de Leon, 1904), reprinted New York 1971
A Berger	*Die zwanzigjährige Arbeiterinnenbewegung Berlins und ihr Ergebnis*, Berlin 1889
E Bernstein	*Geschichte der Berliner Arbeiterbewegung*, Berlin 1910
A Blos	*Die Frauenfrage im Lichte des Sozialismus*, Dresden 1930
A Blos	*Kommunale Frauenarbeit im Kriege*, Berlin 1917
K D Bracher	*Die Auflösung der Weimarer Republik* (Band 4 der Schriften des Instituts für politische Wissenschaften), Stuttgart-Düsseldorf 1955
L Braun	*Die Frauen und die Politik*, Berlin 1903
L Braun	*Frauenarbeit und Hauswirtschaft*, Berlin 1901
L Braun	*Die Frauenfrage*, Leipzig 1901
G Bremme	*Die politische Rolle der Frau in Deutschland*, (Band 4 der Schriftenreihe des UNESCO-Instituts für Sozialwissenschaften), Köln-Göttingen 1956
H Cunow	*Die Marx'sche Geschichts-, Gesellschafts- und Staatstheorie*, 2 vols, Berlin 1920/1921

E Dolléans &
M Crozier — *Mouvements ouvrier et socialiste 1750-1918 (Angleterre, France, Allemagne, États Unis)*, Paris 1950

E Ehehalt — *Die deutsche Arbeitslosigkeit in der Nachkriegszeit*, Dissertation, Gelnhausen 1932

F Engels — *Die englische Zehnstundenbill*, in Marx-Engels, *Kleineökonomische Schriften*, Berlin 1955

F Engels — *Die Entwicklung des Sozialismus von der Utopie zur Wissenschaft*, Frankfurt/M 1946 *(Socialism: Utopian and Scientific*, in Marx-Engels, *Selected Works*, London 1968)

F Engels — *Der Ursprung der Familie, des Privateigentums und des Staates*, Berlin 1954 *(The Origin of the Family, Private Property and the State*, in Marx-Engels, *Selected Works*, London 1968)

E Eyck — *A History of the Weimar Republic*, I, Cambridge Mass 1962

R Fischer — *Stalin and German Communism*, London 1948

O K Flechtheim — *Die KPD in der Weimarer Republik*, Offenbach/M 1948

A Geyer — *Die Frauenerwerbsarbeit in Deutschland*, Jena 1924

F W Halle — *Die Frau in Sowjetrussland*, Berlin-Vienna-Leipzig 1932

H Heidegger — *Die deutsche Sozialdemokratie und der nationale Staat*, Berlin-Frankfurt/M 1956

E Ihrer — *Die Arbeiterinnen im Klassenkampf*, Hamburg 1898

E Ihrer — *Die Organisation der Arbeiterinnen Deutschlands*, Berlin 1893

R Jaeckel — *Die Stellung des Sozialismus zur Frauenfrage im 19 Jahrhundert*, Dissertation, Potsdam 1904

J Joos — *Die sozialdemokratische Frauenbewegung*, Munchen-Gladbach 1912

M Juchacz — *Sie lebten für eine bessere Welt. Lebensbilder führender Frauen des 19 und 20 Jahrhunderts*, Berlin-Hannover 1955

K Kautsky — *The Erfurt Program*, Chicago 1910

K Kautsky — *Die materialistische Geschichtsauffassung*, Berlin 1927

L Kofler — *Marxistischer oder ethischer Sozialismus*, Bovenden b. Göttingen 1955

M Komarowsky — *Women in the Modern World*, Boston 1953

J Kuczynski — *Die Geschichte der Lage der Arbeiter in Deutschland von 1789 bis in die Gegenwart*, Berlin 1954

H Langerhans — *Partei und Gewerkschaft*, Dissertation, Frankfurt/M 1931

H Lion   *Zur Soziologie der Frauenbewegung*, Berlin 1926
E Lüders   *Arbeiterinnenorganisationen und Frauenbewegung*,
                       Leipzig 1904
K Mandelbaum   *Die Erörterungen innerhalb der deutschen Sozial-
                       demokratie über das Problem des Imperialismus,
                       1895-1914*, Dissertation, Frankfurt/M 1927
E Matthias   *Sozialdemokratie und Nation*, Stuttgart 1952
M Mead   *Male and Female in a Changing World*, New York
                       1959
R Michels   *Political Parties. A Sociological Study of Oligarch-
                       ical Tendencies of Modern Democracy*, London 1915
L Otto-Peters   *Das Recht der Frau auf Erwerb*, Hamburg 1866
N Popowa   *Die Gleichberechtigung der Frau, ihre Stellung in
                       der Sowjet-Union*, Berlin 1948
L Preller   *Sozialpolitik in der Weimarer Republik*, Stuttgart
                       1949
A Rosenberg   *A History of the German Republic*, London 1936
R Schlesinger   *Changing Attitudes in Soviet Russia—The Family*,
                       London 1949
W Schröder   *Geschichte der sozialdemokratischen Parteiorganisa-
                       tion in Deutschland*, Dresden 1912
W Sombart   *Der proletarische Sozialismus* ('Marxismus'), Jena
                       1924
F Stampfer   *Die ersten 14 Jahre der deutschen Republik*, Offen-
                       bach/M 1947
S Suhr   *Die weiblichen Angestellten*, Berlin 1930
W Woytinsky   *Der deutsche Arbeitsmarkt, Ergebnisse der gewerk-
                       schaftlichen Arbeitslosenstatistik 1919-1929*, Berlin
                       1930
W Zepler   *Die Frauen und der Krieg*, Berlin 1916
W Zepler   *Sozialismus und Frauenfrage*, Berlin 1919
C Zetkin   *Die Arbeiterinnen- und Frauenfrage der Gegenwart*,
                       Berlin 1889
C Zetkin   *Zur Frage des Frauenwahlrechts*, Berlin 1907
L Zietz   *Die Frauen und die Politik*, Berlin 1912

Index

Complete list of
Pluto books available from:
Pluto Press Ltd, Unit 10 Spencer Court,
7 Chalcot Road, London NW1 8LH

In the USA, from:
Urizen Books Inc, 66 West Broadway,
Suite 406, New York, NY 10007

Sheila Rowbotham

Hidden from History:

300 years of women's oppression
and the fight against it

An account of the changing position of women in England
from the Puritan revolution to the 1930s.
Hidden from History brings together a mass of material
on birth control, abortion and female sexuality; on the complex
relationship of women's oppression and class exploitation and
on the attempts to fuse the struggles against these two.
   Sheila Rowbotham concludes that real equality for women
depends, and has always depended, on 'our capacity to relate to
the working class and the action of working class women in
transforming women's liberation according to their needs'.

paperback/hardback   not for sale in USA

Eli Zaretsky

Capitalism, the Family and Personal Life

The oppression of women rests on an artificial distinction
between work and personal life which capitalism creates and
constantly reinforces. Eli Zaretsky shows how that distinction
divides the sexes and shapes the sense of personal identity.
Zaretsky also shows how that split affected the socialist
movement in the 19th century, how it was reflected in the
Russian and Chinese revolutions and is now reasserting itself in
the debate between radical feminists and traditional socialists.

paperback   not for sale in USA

Victoria Greenwood and Jock Young

Abortion in Demand

When the 1967 Abortion Act released a surge of demand
for abortions in Britain, the abortion law reformers were
acutely embarrassed. The demand came from 'normal', married
women as well as from the social and psychological casualties
they had expected and wished to cater for. It therefore
threatened their view of marriage, of the family and of the role
and attitudes of women. It also provided grounds for a popular
backlash organised by the anti-abortionists and those who share
the reformers' views of society but who fear the effect of their
reforms.

Victoria Greenwood and Jock Young trace the history
and impact of abortion law reform in Britain and explain the
ideological import of moves and counter-moves on the
issue both inside and outside parliament. They stand
uncompromisingly for the untrammelled right of women
to control their own fertility, to choose abortion if they wish,
or to bear children in circumstances that make rearing them a
creative act not a burden.

paperback